SHAPE YOUR SWING THE MODERN WAY

SHAPE YOUR SWING THE MODERN WAY

BY
BYRON NELSON
With LARRY DENNIS

Introduction by Tom Watson
Illustrated by Anthony Ravielli

A GOLF DIGEST BOOK
Distributed by Simon & Schuster

PHOTO CREDITS
Chuck Brenkus, p. 24 (right)
Golf Digest staff, pp. 16-21, 28-31
Will Hertzberg, p. 35 (bottom right),
　p. 38 (bottom right)
Leonard Kamsler, p. 38 (left)
E. D. Lacey, p. 120
Miami Metro, p. 38 (top right)
Lester Nehamkin, p. 34 (right), p. 111
Anthony Roberts, p. 34 (left),
　p. 35 (bottom left)
Sportapics Ltd., p. 35 (top)
United Press International, p. 24 (left)
John Wettermann, p. 115

All rights reserved, including the right of reproduction in whole or in part in any form. Copyright © 1976 by Golf Digest, Inc.

Published by
Golf Digest, Inc.
495 Westport Avenue
Norwalk, Connecticut 06856

Book Trade distribution by
Simon & Schuster
Rockefeller Center
630 Fifth Avenue
New York, New York 10020

First Printing
ISBN: 0-914178-08-3
Library of Congress: 76-264
Manufactured in the United States

INTRODUCTION

My relationship with Byron Nelson began at the Winged Foot Country Club in Mamaroneck, N.Y. in 1974. I had just shot a disastrous 79 in the final round of the U.S. Open, after leading at the end of the third round, and I wasn't feeling very good.

I was sitting in the locker room afterward with John Mahaffey when Byron came over and asked if he could talk to me for a minute.

We went off into a corner and Byron told me that almost every golfer he ever knew had, at some time in his career, suffered exactly what I had just experienced. The pressure had gotten to them and they'd started swinging poorly. He went on to explain to me what, from his vantage point, had happened to my game in that last round. My knees were not working through the shot, he told me, so that I was coming out of the shot too soon and lifting up. I was also staying on my right side too long and wasn't moving well to the left side with my knees flexed.

Looking back on it, I realize that Byron probably took an interest in me because I kind of swing the same way he did. I have a slight dip in my swing and my knees stay flexed throughout the swing. Anyway, after his talk with me I went out and worked on the practice tee and discovered how right he was! My knees weren't working well through the shot at all. I quickly made an adjustment and two weeks later I won the Western Open.

Byron gave me another tip after the 1975 U.S. Open. He told me that I was always going to have a fast swing, but when it got too fast I should slow down the movement of my feet as I took my stance. That would slow everything down, he said, including my swing. And it helped. I kept referring back to it when I got into the heat of the British Open, which I won later that year.

I guess it must be obvious by now that I think Byron Nelson has a tremendous knowledge of the golf swing and the golf game—a knowledge that he willingly shares not just with professionals like myself, but with average weekend golfers. That knowledge is well represented in this book, which is filled with Byron Nelson insights on how to play the game. The images that he gives you are clear and understandable.

More than that, I enjoyed *reading* the book. I especially liked the way Byron describes the evolution of his own swing, and how it became the modern swing. When it comes to golf, I'm a real history buff—and when you read the words of a guy who *is* history, it's exciting. I know you'll find Byron Nelson's book exciting, too. —Tom Watson

PREFACE

I first saw Byron Nelson in the late 1940s when he played an exhibition in my home town of Marshalltown, Iowa. He was officially retired from the professional golf tour by then, although he was to win two more tournaments in the years that followed. But the talent that had made him the greatest of a brief era had not diminished. Even considering that I had watched through a high school teenager's eyes, his skills were awesome.

How good was Byron Nelson? Jug McSpaden, a close friend and traveling companion of Nelson's, observed just a few years ago, "Byron was, and still is, one of the greatest drivers in the history of golf, and beyond question he's the best 2-wood player who ever lived."

Bobby Jones once said, "At my best, I never came close to the golf Nelson shoots."

And Tommy Armour, another golf immortal, observed, "Nelson plays golf shots like a virtuoso. He is the finest golfer I have ever seen."

During the mid-40s, especially during that magical year of 1945, Nelson played the game better than anyone ever has. In 1945 he won 11 tournaments in a row and a total of 18 for the year, records that likely will never be touched. Despite poorly conditioned courses and equipment that was inferior to today's, Byron averaged an incredible 68.33 strokes a round for that memorable season. Nobody ever has equalled his record.

It was more than 20 years after that long-ago exhibition in Iowa that I saw Byron again—and actually met him for the first time. It was May, 1972, at the Byron Nelson Classic in Dallas. We shared in the televised presentation of Golf Digest's Byron Nelson Award to Lee Trevino, the man who had won more professional golf tournaments in 1971 than any other player.

Byron had long since played his last competitive round—the French Open in 1955 was his final victory—but he had remained active in golf. While not tending his 750-acre Fairway Ranch in Roanoke, Tex., he had been busy through the years as a television commentator for ABC, an instruction writer and advisor for *Golf Digest* magazine, a consultant for Northwestern Golf Company, an advisor to the True-Temper Corporation in the development of golf shafts, a golf course designer, a member of the Lincoln-Mercury Sports Panel, a golf tournament (his own) administrator and a sought-after speaker. He remains involved in all these pursuits today.

He has also been a teacher of note. Among his star pupils was Ken Venturi, whom Nelson tutored as an amateur and helped develop into a U.S. Open champion and one of the tour's great stars for a brief, flaming period. Tony Lema, Harvie Ward and Bobby Nichols were also among the successful players who have been helped by Nelson.

Still today, around the practice tees on the professional tour, I see Byron Nelson being asked for and dispensing advice—the same brand of good common sense he gave to Tom Watson after the 1974 U.S. Open. His swing tips are requested from fledgling and star alike; indeed, his phone rings constantly with calls from amateurs of all handicap levels seeking lessons for themselves or for their sons and daughters.

Since that 1972 meeting I have spent time with Nelson on several occasions because of our common work for *Golf Digest*. With each meeting I have become more aware of the depth of his knowledge. But it wasn't until we began to work on this book together that I learned how thoroughly he really understands the golf swing. Closeted for two days with Byron in a hotel room at the Dallas-Fort Worth airport, I became increasingly amazed at his ability to transform sound thoughts into clear, vivid imagery. He paints word pictures that enable you to visualize clearly in your mind what your golf swing should look and feel like. There is no facet of the golf swing or of competitive play that he has not analyzed logically and thoroughly. He can speak instantly and at length on any golf subject. Our taping sessions in Texas lasted less than 12 hours. Yet in that brief time Byron produced enough material to fill three volumes the size of this one.

The result, I think, is a remarkable book. It is pure Nelson, written as he talks, in his easy, down-home style that is at once understandable and entertaining. He tells the story of the evolution of his own swing, which became *the* modern swing as golf passed from the era of wooden to steel shafts. He strips away the mysteries and confusion that have always surrounded the swing, and he tells how to put your new swing to work on the golf course.

What we have, then, is a rare gem—an instruction book that not only will help your game but is also fun to read.

I know it was fun to help write it. You may not derive the benefit, as I did, of tasting Louise Nelson's asparagus casserole—truly a gourmet delight—but you certainly will appreciate the benefits of better, more enjoyable golf by reading this book.

—Larry Dennis
Huntington, Conn.
January, 1976

CONTENTS

Introduction	5
Preface	6

**PART I: THE MODERN SWING—
HOW IT ALL BEGAN** 11

CHAPTER 1: A BETTER WAY TO SWING
A GOLF CLUB 12
   The modern swing catches on 23
   Breaking the psychological barrier 26

CHAPTER 2: TODAY'S STARS AND YOU 32

**PART II: NEW TECHNIQUES TO
CORRECT OLD HABITS** 41

CHAPTER 3: LEARN TO SWING
THE MODERN WAY 43
   The grip 44
   Aim and alignment 46
   Posture 48
   Starting the swing 50
   The backswing 52
   The downswing 54

CHAPTER 4: IMAGES TO MAKE THE
MODERN SWING WORK 56
   Don't be anxious at the top 56
   Be firm but relaxed at the top 57
   Let the right elbow swing free 58
   Keep your arm speed steady 60
   Tempo produces power 61
   Balance marks a good player 63
   Lead the downswing with a free left side 66
   Don't try to hit it 66
   Freedom down below keeps the head still 67
   Swing out from under your head 70
   Stay down and through 71

CHAPTER 5: SPECIAL THOUGHTS TO
DEVELOP POWER AND CONSISTENCY 74
   Hang on with the left hand for consistency 74
   Visualize your target 74
   If you swing harder, stand closer 74
   On taking divots and getting backspin 75
   Woods vs. irons 75
   The full swing is the same with all clubs 75
   The clubhead travels from inside to
along the line 77
   Hit the back of the ball 77
   Hit from the ball on through 79
   Hook from an open face 79
   You must repeat your swing to score well 81

CHAPTER 6: NEW TECHNIQUES TO
MODERNIZE YOUR OLD SHORT GAME 83
   Putting
   Chipping and pitching 91
   Sand play 95
   Unusual lies and trouble shots 99
CHECKPOINTS FOR PART II 104

**PART III: USING YOUR HEAD TO
LOWER YOUR SCORE** 107

CHAPTER 7: THINK YOUR WAY
TO SUCCESS 108
   Be realistic 108
   Play within yourself 110
   Don't think about mechanics 112
   Play with decision 113
   Be aggressive 113
   Strategy is thinking 114

CHAPTER 8: LEARN THE TWO Cs—
CONCENTRATION AND COMPOSURE 117

CHAPTER 9: WHAT MAKES A
CHAMPION 122
   The key to good practice habits 123

EPILOGUE: WHAT HAS HAPPENED
AND WHAT LIES AHEAD 126
Byron Nelson's career record 128

PART I:
THE MODERN SWING— HOW IT ALL BEGAN

CHAPTER 1: A BETTER WAY TO SWING A GOLF CLUB

All I was trying to do was find a better way to swing so I could make a living at the game. I found a better way and, as a result, I've been credited by most experts with developing the modern way to play golf. But I sure wasn't thinking about that at the time.

I started playing golf in 1925, when I was 13 years old and a caddie at Glen Garden Country Club in Fort Worth, Texas. I lived right out close to the golf course and I got to know another boy who caddied there. He lived across town and we went to different schools, so I never saw him except at the golf course—but I saw plenty of him there. His name was Ben Hogan.

Ben and I tied for the caddie championship at Glen Garden one year, when we were 14 or 15. We tied at 40 on the first nine holes, which was a par-37, and the members made us play another nine holes. I shot 39 and Ben shot 40.

I hadn't caddied more than a year or so when the golf pro took an interest in me and gave me a job in the shop cleaning clubs. We used to have to buff the clubs with an abrasive compound, because they didn't have chrome on them the way they do now.

When I was 16 and shooting in the 70s, the club gave me a junior membership. They gave Ben one at the same time. Years later, when we were both grown and had become champions—I was the U.S. Open champion by then—the club threw a big party for us and gave us both honorary lifetime memberships. But a lot had happened in the meantime.

Back in those early days I had the typical old caddie swing. The hickory shafts I used then in my iron clubs had a lot of torque, or twist, in them. So you had to roll the clubface open on the backswing, then roll it closed coming through the shot. If you didn't, the force of your swing would leave the face open when you struck the ball. Naturally, you had to swing flatter, because you couldn't roll the clubface open and swing upright at the same time, the way we do today.

So the swing was loose and flat. "Turn in a barrel" we called it. There wasn't the foot and leg action you see today. The feet were kept pretty flat, and coming through we would hit against a straight left leg and side, kind of throwing the clubface into the ball to get it square again.

That swing worked pretty well with the

irons. But all this time I was using steel-shafted woods and was hooking them something terrible. I never could figure out why. Then, about 1930, I got my first set of steel-shafted irons, and I began hooking with them as badly as I had with my woods.

I realized finally that the reason I was hooking was because the shaft didn't have as much torque, but my hands were still opening and closing as much as ever—pronating and supinating are the technical terms for this. I was rolling the steel-shafted club closed too quickly, and this was causing me to hook the ball.

When I discovered what was happening, I decided not to roll my hands so much. But I was still using that old caddie swing—low and around the shoulders. And I couldn't play as consistently. I'd play a 67 or 68, and all of a sudden I'd shoot 75 or 76 or 77. I didn't know where the clubhead was or what it was doing. I couldn't hit the ball as far, either, and I didn't like that at all.

Everybody else was in the same boat at the time, and nobody knew exactly what to do, but I kept on thinking. I decided that if I were going to take the club back without any pronation, then I'd have to start swinging more upright. So I began taking my hands back higher. But I was still using my feet and legs in the old way—which is to say not much at all—and that didn't work very well.

Then I decided I had to learn to take the club straight back. When I got to the top of the backswing, I felt as if I would just let it fall, with my feet and legs helping to carry it straight back through the ball and keeping it on line toward the target. This would eliminate the hook that was troubling me.

About that time I also developed the idea that I had to keep my head still, and with that discovery everything began to fall into place. Keep my head still . . .take the club right straight back through the ball . . . keep my feet and legs very active, leading the club and helping me carry it through the hitting area . . . keep the legs going straight through toward the target instead of doing any twisting . . . just back and through.

I started making this change in my swing in 1930, when I was 18 years old, but it sure didn't happen all at once. I hit a lot of golf balls trying to make it work. One thing that helped me was practicing against the Texas wind. Keeping the ball down against the wind helped me learn to take the club straight back and

Byron Nelson tees off in the 1935 Masters at the famed Augusta National course, where he later won the championship in 1937 and 1942.

straight through. I also think my pronounced leg drive developed from trying to keep the ball low against the wind. I was trying to swing through the ball with as shallow an arc as possible at the bottom and keep the club going down the target line as long as I could. You need strong leg action to do that.

In fact, I received criticism for years from players who were still swinging the old way. They said I stayed down too low through the ball, that I had a dip in my swing, that my foot and leg action was too loose. In a way, they were right. I almost overdid it. My foot and leg action was even looser than what they use now. I don't think many people could play as loose-kneed as I did. But it worked for me; besides, all that criticism didn't worry me as long as I was cashing those checks regularly.

At any rate, I think I was the first player to make the complete change from the old way of swinging to the modern method we use today. Of course, the older players weren't making many changes, even with the steel shafts. They had played their way for so long that they probably were afraid to. As we get older, we tend to resist change.

But I feel the younger players did start to copy me. Most people, I guess, like to copy somebody who is successful, and after a while I began to have pretty good success with that swing.

I turned professional in November, 1932, went to Texarkana, and played in a little $500 tournament there with Dick Metz, Ky Laffoon and people like that. I finished third and won $75. I was 20 years old by then.

The next spring they hired me as the pro at Texarkana Country Club. There was so little money in the tournaments back in those days that you had to make your living at a club. In fact, the only time I ever stayed on tour full time was in 1945 until the day I quit in August 1946. I stayed two years at Texarkana, was an assistant in 1935 and 1936 at Ridgewood (N.J.) Country Club, spent three years at Reading Country Club in Pennsylvania and was the pro at Inverness in Toledo from 1940 until 1946.

I began playing in tournaments right away, though. In 1933 I tried to play in two or three without any money and ended up hitch-hiking back home from California. I returned to the winter tour that fall, but in the summer of 1934 I played in only a few local tournaments. By then I had made enough of a

The famed Byron Nelson swing shows Nelson in a balanced, relaxed address posture (#1), his arms hanging freely. His 4-wood swings straight back from the ball (#2) and moves gradually inside (#3); cocking of the wrists begins when the hands are about hip-high (#4).

Nelson swings the club into a perfect square position at the top, the club on a plane parallel to the target line (#6). Nelson's first move down is with the lower left side (#7); his wrists remain cocked and his power is stored until well into the forward swing (#8).

Through the impact area, Nelson's club stays on the target line longer than most players' and is just beginning to move back inside as the ball speeds away (#9 and 10). Note that he stays "down and through" the shot. While his head remains steady, his arms and club appear to be chasing the ball toward the target until he completes the swing in a full, high finish (#11 and 12).

reputation so that I was invited to the second Masters tournament. As it turned out, that was very fortunate for me.

Ed Dudley, who later became president of the Professional Golfers' Association, was the pro at Augusta National then. George Jacobus, the head pro at Ridgewood and president of the PGA at that time, told Ed that he was looking for a young man who had some promise to be his assistant. Ed referred my name to him and I went to work for George at Ridgewood in 1935.

My job was to work in the shop, play with the members some and teach. George developed an interest in me and was very helpful. He was a good teacher and taught me a lot of things about teaching. More important, he agreed to help me with my game. I had talked with George about the new method I was using, and, even though he was teaching the old way of playing, he agreed with me 100 percent that I was on the right track.

Often when I practiced, George would check several things in my swing that I felt were important. Was I keeping the club on line? Was I keeping my head still? Was I keeping my knees and legs moving on the same plane that paralleled the one the club should be on?

At the time, I felt my lower body move was a simple lateral thrust toward the target. I didn't realize I was turning my hips as much as I was. Your hips must turn, of course, but because I had always turned mine against a straight left side, I now felt like my action had become all feet and legs.

I used my feet a great deal. When I came into the ball, it seemed as though I was driving off my right foot, and in the impact area I felt that I almost gave a shove off that foot. But I always made sure my weight stayed on the inside of the right foot on the backswing. I never let it get to the outside.

I started playing in local tournaments around that area. In 1936 I won the Metropolitan Open at Quaker Ridge in Scarsdale, N.Y. I played very well and very steady in it, which I hadn't been doing up to that time, and that gave me the confidence that what I was doing was right.

So I kept working on this theory of keeping the face of the club square with the back of the left hand, just as though I was trying to hit the ball with the back of that hand.

I felt I was controlling the swing from the left side. But I knew I was getting some power from the right side, not early in the swing, but late. That was something that just kind of happened. I wouldn't recommend that anyone deliberately try to hit with the right side, because if you do you'll be in trouble. Even though I felt I pushed off the right foot, I don't believe you should think about this, because you'll do it too much ahead of time. The right-side power builds up because of the proper use of the feet and legs. When you move to the right in the backswing and then back to the left, you automatically generate the proper use of the right side.

Finally, in 1937, I had developed this style of play to my satisfaction, and to George's, too. I also started winning consistently that year: I won the Masters and three other tournaments, and I played on the Ryder Cup team. I never tried to change anything in my swing from that time on.

THE MODERN SWING CATCHES ON

There were some great players before me who did some of the things I tried to do with my swing. Gene Sarazen was one. He swung a little flat because he was short, but in the later years of his playing career he took the club back very straight on line and swung it back quite high for a little fellow. He had somewhat of an open position—that is, he lined up a little left of the target, the way most good players do today—and he stayed "under" the ball real well.

Walter Hagen was pretty close to a modern swinger. He was very much a hands player and didn't use his feet and legs so much, but he didn't do much pronating and got his hands up good and high on the backswing.

Hogan, of course, made a decided swing change in mid-career, and he has added greatly to the knowledge of the golf swing. Ben started out as a player who hooked the ball, and why he did that is an interesting story. When we were caddying at Glen Garden, there weren't as many members as there are now, and while we were waiting for caddying jobs we would hit balls up and down the driving range.

We caddies would line up and all hit the same club, and the one who hit the ball the shortest had to retrieve all the balls. Ben was pretty slight in those days. But the ground was hard—this

Three legendary golfers who played about the same time as Nelson—Sam Snead (left), Gene Sarazen (below, left) and Ben Hogan (below)—embodied many or most of the modern swing characteristics. Note Sarazen's flatter follow-through, typical of the earlier players. He later learned with much success to swing the club back straight and high. Hogan, who has contributed greatly to the knowledge of the game, made a mid-career swing change that put him in tune with modern principles.

was before watered fairways—and if you could hook the ball and get it rolling it would go a long way.

Ben soon found out that if he turned his left hand over to the right and got in a strong position and swung fairly flat, he could hook the ball and hit it long enough so he wouldn't have to chase the balls. That's the way he learned, and he did reasonably well on the tour playing that way. He practiced constantly and he learned to repeat his swing every time.

Shortly after the war, he weakened his grip some—turned it more to the left on the club—and began swinging more uprightly. As a matter of fact, Ben was the one who started breaking his wrists right away on the backswing, then holding and carrying the club on up with his arms and shoulders the way Johnny Miller, Tom Watson and Lanny Wadkins do today.

It was almost two separate moves with Ben, more so than the boys I've just mentioned. They use a modified version of Hogan's. And these changes helped Ben become a very straight driver. He could drive it right down the pike, which is probably the reason why he went on to become a four-time U.S. Open winner.

Ben never lacked for distance, either. Even with the new swing, he drove the ball a long way. He was always quite thin; he had small hips and legs, but his legs were strong and he had large hands and arms. He used them well. He also was a player who kept his head very still and never let it move past the ball. He never shanked. I only remember seeing Hogan shank the ball once and it frightened him, because he'd never done it before. He always kept his head in back of the ball through the shot. Letting the head go past the ball is one of the main reasons for the shank, because when you do that you have to swing around yourself. Then you're in trouble.

The modern players have carried the improvements in the swing even further, I feel. They tie the whole swing together better than I did. They combine the use of their feet and legs with the whole turn of their bodies.

They stand reasonably close to the ball—closer than we did in my time—and they push the club straight back. Even if some of them break their wrists immediately, they hold it, and by the turn of their shoulders they carry the club high into the air. They make a big shoulder turn, but they don't let their hips turn as much as the shoulders. As a group, the players today get their hands much higher on the backswing than I did. Over the years they have developed a longer, fuller arc, a fuller extension going back and coming through. And they do it more smoothly.

As a result, they hit the ball harder and farther, yet they hit it amazingly straight. They do this because they have such good control of the left side. I don't know of a good player out there today who doesn't control his swing with the left side. They also keep the club more on line with the target during the swing, and they keep their heads very still.

In my era, we were not taught that you had to hold your head still. Perhaps it wasn't as necessary for the players then, because they didn't have to be so careful about keeping the ball on the fairway. Even though the fairways were just as narrow then as they are now, most players weren't driving the ball as far. When you're driving it 255 yards as the boys are today, you've got to be straighter to keep it in the fairway than when you're hitting it only 225 or 235. It's simply a matter of angle.

That's why I tried to keep my head still. And that's why I kept complete control in the left side, the left hand and arm, never letting that clubhead get past my hands until I'd passed the hitting area. After I made my swing change, I began to drive the ball about as long as most of them do now—but I had to do those things in order to stay on the fairways.

BREAKING THE PSYCHOLOGICAL BARRIER

One big reason the players today hit it farther and straighter is their attitude. When I was growing up, we were taught that if you tried to hit the ball hard you wouldn't be able to keep it on the fairway and you would lose some finesse around the green.

Oh, there were some long hitters in my time. Jimmy Thomson was one, of course. But it seemed as if the long hitters then only worked on one thing, and that was hitting the ball hard. That thinking began to change a bit during the 1940s, because along came people like Sam Snead, who hit the ball long as well as straight.

It really wasn't until the Arnold Palmer era that the whole psychology of scoring changed. Here was a man who slashed at the ball and drove it a mile, but he putted like gang-busters, too. The good players began to realize that they could do it all—that they could drive the ball long and straight and play with finesse around the greens. It's like running the mile in four minutes or pole-vaulting 18 feet. As soon as you believe it can be done, a great psychological barrier is broken and you begin to work toward higher goals. That's what the players started to do after Arnold showed them the way, and that's what they do today.

There is no question that improvements in equipment have helped. The sand wedge particularly has lowered scores, because now shots can be played out of sand or from rough around the greens without fear. In my day you had to play them with a mashie or a mashie-niblick, which took lots of touch and finesse. Nowadays players know that with the sand wedge and the modern swing—getting those hands nice and high and keeping the wrists firm through the short shots—they can put the ball just about where they want it. If they can swing at it, they feel they can get it close to the hole, and this attitude has been a tremendous help in lowering scores. Working hard, particularly on their short game, has also made a big difference, because they really work at it.

So the whole psychology has changed. It probably began with Snead and Hogan and me, but the players today have carried our thinking forward a long way.

Swinging a 3-iron, Nelson takes the club away in "one piece," his left side in control (#1 and 2). His weight shifts to his right but remains on the inside of the right foot, his knees still flexed (#3). At the top, he is in perfect balance; his left arm is firm, and the back of his left hand and forearm are in a solid, square position (#4). His club is far short of horizontal, but his big shoulder turn has fully coiled his upper body. He is behind the ball and ready to make a smooth, powerful forward swing.

Nelson's forward swing is initiated with the movement of his left knee toward the target (#5 and 6). As he swings through impact and beyond, his knees stay well flexed in the classic Nelson leg drive (#7 and 8). Note the solid position of his left arm and hand at impact and how his head remains in a relatively steady position until after the ball is long gone.

CHAPTER 2: TODAY'S STARS AND YOU

I find it fascinating to watch the good players of today and analyze what they do that makes them good. There are some whose styles I wouldn't recommend for the average player, but you could help your game a great deal by watching most of them.

All of the great players today do several things in common. They are in a good position when standing at the ball, they stay in good balance during their swing, and they keep a straight left arm as they bring the club straight back and through the ball. Because they keep their heads still and in back of the ball during the swing, and because they swing underneath themselves, they all get the ball nicely into the air.

I've also found that all champions play well "within themselves," rather than going "all out" every time. I remember doing a telecast with the ABC crew at the Andy Williams-San Diego tournament one year. We were watching play at the 16th hole at Torrey Pines, a good par-3. Nicklaus and his group were coming up, and somebody said that he'd bet Nicklaus would use a shorter club than anybody else. I told him that I thought he'd be surprised, that Jack would use as long a club as anybody else and probably longer. The other two players tried to reach the green with 6-irons. Nicklaus used a 4-iron, made a good comfortable swing and knocked the ball right up to the pin.

My companions were amazed, but they shouldn't have been. The fine player will never hit the ball as hard as he has to—*until* he has to. Otherwise, he'll disrupt his concentration on making a good swing, lose control and wear himself out before the day is over.

A LOOK AT SOME OF THE STARS

One of the best actions among the modern players belongs to Gene Littler. Everybody should try to emulate him, because Gene's tempo is smooth and easy and he doesn't ever try to force a shot. He swings within himself all the time. He doesn't rush when he's walking or at any other time. He talks medium slow, he walks medium slow, he stands at the ball in a very comfortable position and he swings medium slow. There is not much that Gene Littler doesn't do medium slow.

If you feel you can swing a little stronger than Gene does, I would say you would do well to pattern yourself after Nicklaus—particularly if you're built on the stocky side, the way Jack is. Of course, Jack is one of the great players of all time, if not the greatest. He takes a very comfortable position at the ball, doesn't rush his swing, doesn't do anything bad at all. He's firm, without any looseness in his hands and arms throughout his swing. He keeps his head remarkably still and he allows the club to be swung back and carried to the top of the backswing into a very high but firm position.

He turns his body well. When you examine his position at the top of the swing, he seems to be almost squatting slightly in relation to his starting position. He looks like a cat ready to spring. From there he moves very decidedly. The club comes down close to his body—not out and around but dropping down close to the right side. Then he carries the club through with a beautiful flowing action of the left side, the legs leading all the way through the swing. And he has a beautiful, high follow-through and finish, which is a direct result of what he has done earlier in his swing.

Now then, if you're a tall fellow, I would suggest that you try to emulate somebody like Tom Weiskopf. He has excellent rhythm. He stands at address in a natural position with his arms hanging down freely. Tom doesn't turn at the hips quite as much as some of the shorter players, but he has a beautiful shoulder turn and carries the club nice and high on the backswing. He gets the club just about to the horizontal position on the backswing, and because of this he has a very full, flowing arc. He gets the ball up in the air beautifully and hits it a mile. Yet he can grip down on the club, squat down a bit and play delicate, little short shots.

If you're a smaller fellow, you might look to someone like Tom Kite. Tom is a younger player who is doing quite well and has a great future. His arms are not very long but he makes good use of his body to help him get enough arc. A smaller player has to get some arc to hit the ball far enough to keep up with the taller players, and the way to do this is to get your body moving. On the backswing, Kite moves from his left foot right up through his shoulders, in controlled fashion. When he comes through the shot, his legs are leading and his body is helping to carry his armswing. He really moves through the ball, which is a point I'm going to re-emphasize later on.

Although each has his own individual style, the top players pictured here all swing the modern way. Jack Nicklaus (below), Gene Littler (right), and on the opposite page Tom Watson (above), Tom Weiskopf (below, left) and Johnny Miller all adhere to the modern swing fundamentals: carrying the club longer down the target line, greater use of the lower body, and playing with power, yet "within themselves."

Johnny Miller is another great player who moves fast through the ball. As a matter of fact, he goes through so fast that he shifts clear over onto the outside of his left foot, maybe too far. But his balance is so great and he keeps his head so still that it doesn't affect him adversely. He may fall off balance occasionally, but only after the shot has been completed.

Arnold Palmer doesn't swing the club as uprightly or get his hands as high as most of the players I've mentioned. He stands quite a distance away from the ball, and as a result he swings flatter. But he has been able to overcome this fault by the great use of his feet and legs through the hitting area. Also, he has such strong arms and hands that he never lets the club turn over, which would cause him to pull or hook. He carries the club right straight through the shot and even moves his head a little so as not to let the club come on around.

I guess if you wanted to nitpick you could find something wrong with nearly everybody's swing. But Palmer has been such an exceptional player because there are so many good things about his swing—especially his strength, the great use of his feet and legs and the fact that he never lets the clubhead pass his hands in the hitting area. In the days when he was winning, he just never did. Therefore, even though he didn't fade the ball, he didn't hook it enough to cause himself any problems.

There are a lot of different ways to strike a golf ball well, as long as you observe certain fundamentals. Palmer is an example of this. So is Lee Trevino. He has a rather peculiar action, but it works for him. In the first place, he has one of the greatest pair of hands I've ever seen. I've always felt Lee could have been a surgeon. Just by the way he puts his hands on the club you know that he's got control of it at all times.

Trevino keeps his left arm very straight throughout the swing. He has a decidedly open stance, and he takes the club straight up and away from the ball. He doesn't take the club inside the line at all until he gets to the top, and then it drops a little bit inside as he starts down. He uses the old theory of moving onto the left side and through the ball with the legs straight; but he also uses some of the modern theory by staying way under with the right side. His left side comes up and his right side kind of comes under. He never lets the club come over the top, pulling across the line and closing the face—and that's why he fades the ball and is so beautifully accurate.

I love Lee's action, and I can understand why he plays so well. But I do think it would be difficult for the average person to play the way he does. It requires great skill and tremendous dedication, and not everybody has those qualities to the degree Trevino does.

I feel I should mention something about Bruce Crampton, both for what he does and doesn't do. Bruce is another player who gets his hands very high, but he doesn't seem to turn as much as Nicklaus and some of the others. They turn their bodies enough so that their arms and clubs have time to get in the proper groove. But Bruce appears to use just an arm swing. He takes the club almost straight up, and his left wrist gets into somewhat of a cupped or broken position. Something has to complete the backswing, and this is the way he does it—rather than with a good full turn of the shoulders, like a Nicklaus or a Palmer.

I think this tendency has caused Bruce some problems on occasion and, frankly, I think it's one reason he hasn't won a major championship up to this point. There is more pressure and more tension involved in winning a national championship than a regular tournament. If you haven't turned as much as you should, and if you're too tense and too quick starting down, you'll swing outside the target line and come over the top of the ball. That's what happens to Bruce, plus the fact that he doesn't use his feet and legs as much as some of the other modern players. It all causes him to pull the ball sometimes, or to block it and push it right.

I don't mean to sound that critical of Bruce. He's a million-dollar winner who certainly is capable of winning a major championship at any time. But if there's one thing Bruce should remember about his game, it is to turn his shoulders a little more, get the club more in back of him and not quite so high.

As far as I'm concerned, Gary Player is the best world player today. He wins on courses all over the globe, and in doing this he shows a remarkable ability to adjust. It takes a lot of self-discipline to do this—to win under so many different conditions. It also takes an ability to know what you can do physically and mechanically with your golf swing. I've seen Gary make some significant changes in his game during the course

The swing techniques of these all-time greats—Arnold Palmer (below), Gary Player (right) and Lee Trevino (below, right)—illustrate that there is more than one way to strike a golf ball well. Although each player has his own individual style, they all observe the same basic fundamentals of the modern swing.

of a championship. The average champion wouldn't dare do this, but Gary has the self-discipline to carry it off successfully.

He sometimes looks like he's losing his balance when he swings, but during his backswing and all through the hitting area he is very steady. He keeps his head still and has a very firm left side—it's like a ramrod that never gives way. His hands grip the golf club with great strength; he doesn't ever let it get away from him.

Gary has realized that he doesn't have the size— he's only 5′8″ and 150 pounds—to give him enough natural distance, so he has worked on his body, developing tremendous muscle power and utilizing every possible ounce of strength. That in itself requires extraordinary discipline. To keep himself in top physical shape, Gary does everything else in moderation because he realizes that with so little natural physical ability this is necessary. His attitude is one we all could profit by, whether we are playing for international championships, as Gary is, or simply struggling to win a title at our own club.

So far I have explained to you the swing that I helped to develop and, as I see it, the swing that the great players are using now. Obviously, I believe the best way to play golf is with the modern swing. It's much better than the swing we used when I first started in the game. It certainly works for me—and it definitely can work for you.

During the years I have spent playing, teaching and observing, I have developed some thoughts that I feel will help any player understand the modern golf swing more clearly and help him perform it more effectively. In the following chapters, I will pass along these thoughts and explain my ideas on how to swing at the ball and make a good score. I firmly believe these points will add immeasurably to your ability to play well and enjoy what I consider to be the greatest game there is.

PART II: NEW TECHNIQUES TO CORRECT OLD HABITS

CHAPTER 3:
LEARN TO SWING THE MODERN WAY

First, let's examine the fundamentals. Two essential areas make up a good golf swing. The first is the foundation—the basic elements of grip, aim and alignment, posture, waggle and takeaway, backswing, and downswing.

Without building a proper foundation, you can't succeed in the second area, which is the swing itself. And when I say *swing*, I mean just that. For too many people, the golf swing is made up of positions, a series of unrelated movements that get the club from one point to another and back again—sometimes in the right place, usually not.

Remember that in the modern golf swing *ease* and *comfort* are the watchwords. The best way to swing is the simplest way. Most players try to make the golf swing more difficult than it really is. They fiddle around and twist themselves into uncomfortable positions; they force their muscles to make unnatural moves that get them out of position and reduce their chances of hitting the ball solid and straight.

If you are one of those people still struggling along with a complicated swing, please understand there is a better way. By reading the pages that follow, you'll have a clearer picture in your mind of what really happens in a good golf swing. And with that understanding you'll be a better player— because the old habits, doubts and uncertainties that ruined your swing in the past will, with practice, eventually disappear.

Let's turn to those essential swing areas, beginning with the grip.

1. The overlapping grip brings the hands closer together and helps them work as a unit. Left-hand dominance should be felt throughout the swing—at address, to the top of the backswing and right on through completion of the downswing. You should feel firmness in your hands but freedom in your forearms.

THE GRIP: FEEL PRESSURE IN HANDS BUT NOT IN FOREARMS

While there are many factors that go into a good golf swing, the first thing you must learn is to place your hands on the club correctly. It is very difficult to be a good player if you don't have a good grip, yet I see few amateurs who hold the club properly.

I personally prefer the Vardon (or overlapping) grip because it brings the hands closer together on the club. This helps them work more as a unit. Please examine carefully the positioning of the fingers in the drawing on the opposite page. Note that the back of the left hand and the palm of the right are in much the same position as the clubface—that is, facing the target. I always like to feel as if I'm striking the ball with the back of my left hand and the palm of my right.

I've never made a big thing about grip pressure, but there are a couple of guidelines you should be aware of. First, you should grip the club firmly enough so that you *feel pressure in the hands but not in the forearms*. Most players squeeze the club so hard they tighten up the muscles in their forearms. This creates tension and makes it difficult, if not impossible, to take the club away from the ball correctly.

The good player will develop a way of gripping the club firmly in his hands and still leave freedom in his arms. Among the top professionals today, Tom Watson is an excellent example. He clamps his hands on the club with great firmness, but you'll see complete freedom in his hands and wrists, which means he has not built up pressure in his arms.

Second, you should grip the club more firmly in the left hand than in the right. Whatever you do, make sure your left hand dominates your right—or vice-versa if you're a left-hander—from the time you take hold of the club until you finish the swing. If you hold the club with the same pressure in each hand, your naturally stronger right hand will overpower your left and take control of the swing, with disastrous results.

2. At address, keep a slightly open stance. A stance that is closed too far (A) will cause the clubhead to travel from inside the target line and strike the ball to the right; a stance that is too open (B) will create a swing path from outside to inside the target line, causing a pull or slice.

AIM AND ALIGNMENT: KEEP A SLIGHTLY OPEN STANCE

Proper aim and alignment certainly are among the most important factors in striking the ball solid and straight. Maybe they are the most important. If your clubface is not aimed correctly or your body is not aligned properly, you instinctively will try to make some adjustment which usually will result in a mis-hit shot.

One good rule that will help you aim the club and align your body better is this: as you set up to the ball, make sure your eyes are parallel to, or on a line with, your target line. Then swivel your head slightly to the right and look down the line a little more with your left eye. As you check the target, just rotate your head instead of lifting it. Do this with every shot—it will give you better optical alignment and will unconsciously help you improve the alignment of your clubface and body to the target

Now study closely the illustration on the opposite page. Note that all parts—feet, knees, hips, shoulders—are square with each other but set very slightly open or to the left of the target line. The clubface is square to, or pointing directly down, the target line.

This slightly open stance enables you to face more toward the target. It makes it easier for the left side to move out of the way and the right side to come "under" during the downswing. If you stand too closed to the line (*illustration A*), you either will swing the club too much from the inside of the line and strike the ball to the right, or you will feel blocked out from the target and tend to come "over the top" in an attempt to pull the ball back on line. If you are too open (*illustration B*), your swing path will be from outside to inside the target line, causing a pull or slice.

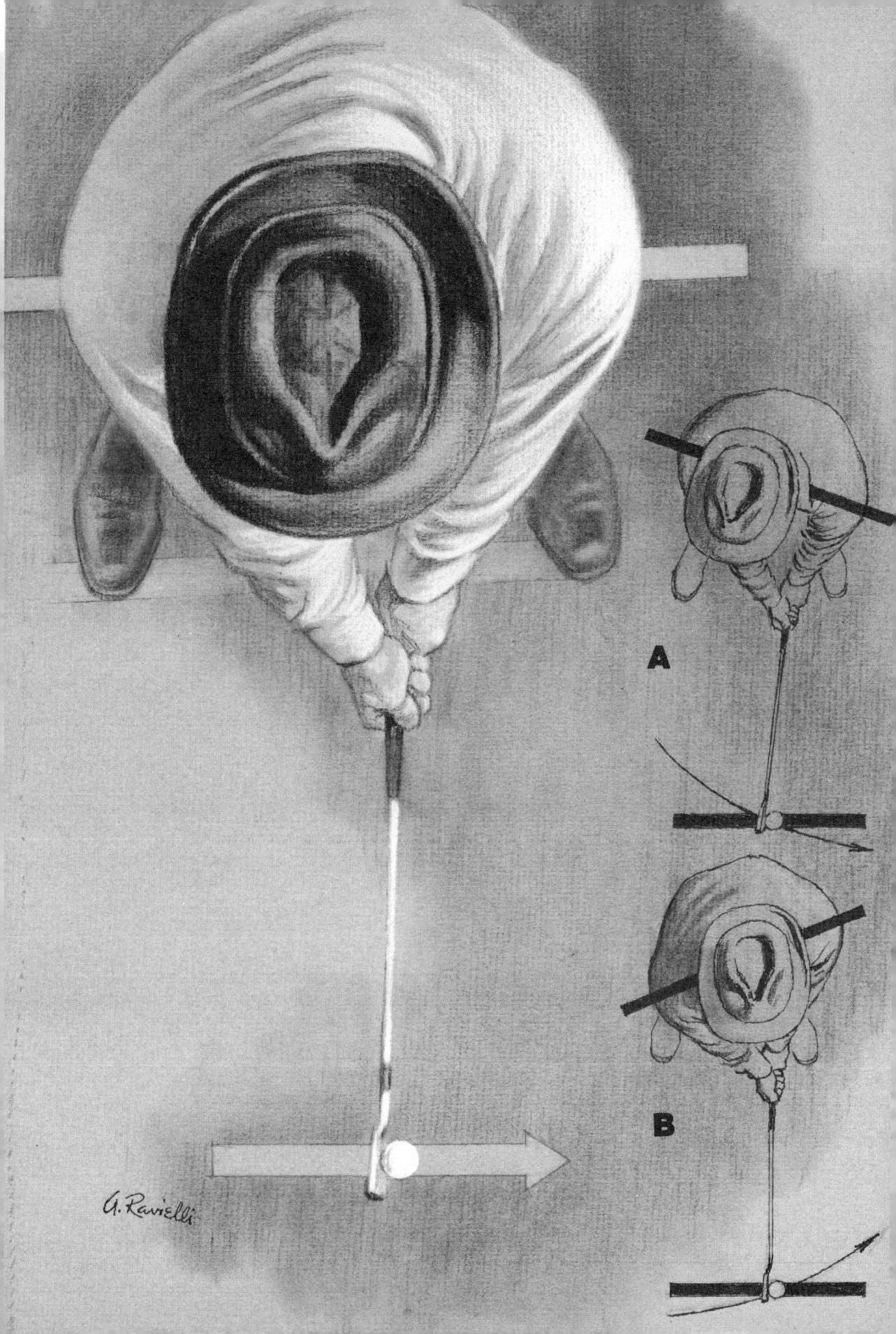

3. Proper posture means good balance, with weight equally distributed and knees flexed slightly to allow free footwork and leg action. The feet are shoulder-width apart at the inside of the heels for a driver shot (right); the left arm is comfortably extended, the right arm and side are relaxed.

POSTURE: BE BALANCED AND COMFORTABLE

Without proper posture, you have little chance of making a good swing. *Illustration #3* (opposite page) shows how proper posture puts you in good balance, with the weight evenly distributed and the knees flexed just enough to allow free footwork and leg action. Your feet should be about shoulder-width apart at the inside of the heels for a driver shot, and you should be bent forward slightly from the hips. Your lower back should be straight and your arms should hang freely rather than reaching for the ball or crowding in too close to it. The left arm should be comfortably extended, the right arm and side relaxed. This places the left side in a slightly higher, leading position. The ball should be positioned in the center of the clubface and played just inside the left heel for iron shots. For drives, it should be placed off the instep or left toe.

I don't think you could find a better model for correct posture than Jack Nicklaus. Anyone who copies him can't help but improve his or her game. To start with, Jack is in absolutely superb balance. His weight is equally distributed between his two feet, perhaps slightly favoring the left. He stations his weight equally between the ball and heel of each foot, and his weight is towards the insides of his feet. There is a slight flex in his knees. He leans neither forward nor back, and he bends just slightly from the hips; his lower back is straight rather than slumped.

I'd like you to copy Nicklaus in one other respect: he positions the center of his clubface smack-dab behind the ball at address. I know you'll see some good players address the ball off the toe or the heel of the club, but doing that demands compensations during the swing which only a practiced, accomplished athlete can make.

4. The takeaway is controlled by the left side. The left shoulder and left arm push the club smoothly away from the ball and high into the air. The relaxed right side is just pushed out of the way. The clubhead leads in the backswing as a result of left-hand control.

STARTING THE SWING: TAKE CLUB AWAY WITH LEFT SIDE

Although the swing actually starts when you take your first step in addressing the ball, the crucial moment comes just before the takeaway on the backswing. It is here that you must make a vital movement called the *waggle*. The main thing to remember is that the waggle is just a little bitty swing that follows along the same path—for maybe a foot or so—that your full swing will travel. It's done mostly with the hands and arms and partly with your feet. You shouldn't be picking your feet up and moving them around unless you're out of position. But once you're properly lined up, you should still move around on your feet a little—almost within your shoes. The waggle sets the tempo for the whole swing, so if you're ever fidgety and jerky with this movement, it's going to be difficult for you to make a smooth swing.

As you complete your waggle and bring the club back to the ball, move smoothly into a *forward press*, which is just a slight movement of the weight to your left. Use your legs, being careful not to move your shoulders and the rest of your body too much. This will throw your clubface out of alignment. The forward press should simply be a slight transfer of weight to the left and then back to the right—a little rocking motion that gets your swing started.

Now take the club smoothly away from the ball on a straight line. How far back you take it depends on your type of swing. I once heard Arnold Palmer say that if he got started right during the first 14 inches of his swing he never had to think about anything else during the rest of it. That may be a slight exaggeration, particularly for a player who has less ability than Arnold, but it illustrates the importance good players place on the takeaway.

If you take the club away wrong, then you must make all sorts of compensations in order to get it back to the ball properly in the hitting area. Unless you make those compensations during the backswing or at the top, you're dead. Even if you do make them, you're treading a dangerous path. Most players don't realize that they are probably going to return the club to the ball in exactly the same position in which they set up to it and took the club away.

I believe that your takeaway should be in one piece. You should feel that you are starting the club back with your whole left side moving together with your left hand and arm. When I was playing my best, I definitely began my takeaway with my left side. You can see this clearly in *illustration #4* (opposite). The left hand is firmly in control. The left shoulder and left arm push the club away from the ball on a straight line for a few inches, then swing it high into the air. The relaxed right side is just pushed out of the way.

5. To reach the top of the backswing, turn the shoulders and swing the arms as far as possible without loosening the grip. Note that the wrists cock gradually until, at the top, they are set in the proper position.

THE BACKSWING: WIND UP FULLY BUT DON'T OVERSWING

The most important thing I can tell you about your backswing is: *don't overswing*. It is absolute nonsense to think that a longer backswing will give you longer shots. Often just the reverse is true. The goal of the backswing is simply to wind up fully and put yourself and the club in position to strike the ball as squarely and forcefully as possible.

There is no standard backswing length that applies to everyone, because some players are more supple than others and can turn their bodies without moving off the ball. When I was younger, I could get my hands nice and high, almost to the point that Nicklaus does, and still not move off the ball. Now my swing arc is a foot and a half shorter.

To reach the top of your backswing, simply turn your shoulders and swing your arms back as far as you can. The length of your backswing depends on how fully you can turn your shoulders and how far you can swing your arms *without* doing any of these things: (1) loosening your grip; (2) moving your head; (3) relaxing and bending your left arm; (4) overcocking or cupping your wrists; (5) going up too far on your left toe. If you swing back as fully as you can without committing any of these errors, you will achieve the normal length of your backswing. These are check points to be used in practice.

Here are some other *must-do's* in the successful backswing formula: Keep the head reasonably still and in position. Keep both hands firmly on the club. Keep the left arm straight—not rigid, but firm and straight. Keep the balance on both feet. Allow the legs to move, but have enough tautness in them to keep them from moving too far.

Note in *illustration #5* (opposite) that the wrists cock gradually during the backswing until, at the top, they are set in the proper position. It's important not to break your wrists too soon, or to drag the club back too far along the ground. Some players start too quickly with their hands and arms and leave their bodies behind. Others drag the clubhead, letting it lag a bit, because they're starting with their bodies.

When you're at the top of the swing the club should be set at whatever stopping position is natural for you. Someone watching your swing should be unable to detect any particular point where your wrists start to cock. Those who do break their wrists too fast and pick the club up at the start tend to stop turning their shoulders. And those who go too far before the break either don't break at all or break too suddenly—causing a whiplash or bounce at the top.

6. *The downswing is a chain reaction, in which the left side pulls the left hand, arm and clubhead down through the shot. But the feeling should be that the entire left side—foot, leg, hip, shoulder and left arm—starts down together as a unit.*

THE DOWNSWING: START EVERYTHING DOWN TOGETHER

I think of the downswing as a kind of chain reaction. The first link in the chain is the left side. It moves into and through the ball, pulling the hands down, into and through. The hands, in turn, pull the clubhead down, into and through the ball. You can observe this sequence in *illustration #6* (opposite) and in *illustration #9*. The feeling should be that the entire left side—foot, leg, hip, shoulder and arm—starts down together, as a unit. Any attempt to start either the legs or the arms first will result in mis-timing that can ruin the swing.

The key to starting the downswing properly is the left knee. During the backswing it moves laterally to the right. Your downswing should begin with this knee, still flexed, returning laterally to the left. This movement will anchor your left heel and cause your legs and lower body to slide to your left, establishing that pulling pattern with your whole left-side arm-hand unit.

As the hips move to the left, the right knee moves toward the ball, allowing the right shoulder to come down and "under" properly. Your weight is moving from the inside of your right heel to the outside of your left heel, where it will be at the finish of your swing. Your left hand is still firmly in control of the club as your left side moves past the ball; your head remains steady in back of the ball; your body is beginning to bow into a reverse-C shape.

After the initial lateral movement, the left leg and hip start to turn out of the way—enough to allow the arms and hands to swing through on the intended target line. The lower left side stays down and through the shot, never coming up. The term "down and through" means that in the impact area the club is still moving on a slightly downward arc. If you are using an iron, strike the ball first and immediately afterward begin to take a divot. If you keep the left side leading and in control in the impact area, you will have no trouble staying down to the shot.

During the swing, I always try to imagine the back of my left hand, left arm, and the face of the club as being one piece, like a ramrod. That way I feel I'm not getting the face opened or closed. I just take this whole unit back and return it squarely to the ball. I might push the ball sometimes or maybe pull it slightly, but there is very little curvature of the ball in the air.

The finish of your swing is just a reflection of what you've done before. I will guarantee a nice, high, well balanced finish if you have: (1) a firm grip; (2) a smooth, rhythmic swing; (3) a package backswing with everything moving as a unit, and (4) a chain-reaction downswing with the left side leading the hands and clubhead down, into and through the ball.

CHAPTER 4: IMAGES TO MAKE THE MODERN SWING WORK

You now have a blueprint for what should be done and what should be felt during the swing, beginning with the grip and extending all the way through impact. In this chapter, you will find a series of thoughts that can help you make those critical movements more effectively and blend them into that new, unified swing we're all after.

The following pages are filled with ideas that you can use to understand, picture, and feel the various parts of the swing as well as the swing in its entirety. By absorbing these ideas and putting them to practical use, you will soon learn the purpose of the modern golf swing and be better able to fit the parts together. If you are a beginner, your game will rest on a more solid foundation. If you have played for some time, but not as well as you'd like, you can get rid of those old-fashioned swing habits that have been holding you back and replace them with a new, winning style.

DON'T BE ANXIOUS AT THE TOP

In the last chapter I talked about the *chain-reaction* downswing—the sequence of motion that occurs starting down from the top. It's important that this be a well-timed sequence. You should have the feeling that the left foot, left knee, left hip and left shoulder all start the downswing together. This leading left side then carries the left arm and hands *down* into the hitting area. The clubhead is being returned to its original position, ready to be released by the hands and wrists at the proper time. This occurs near the bottom of the swing as the momentum of the body pulls everything through.

Obviously, this sequence must be carried out smoothly. The key thought here—and it's one of the most important you'll ever be given—is *don't get too anxious to hit*. Don't try to get the downswing started before the backswing is completed.

If you do get anxious and rush into the downswing, one of two disasters can occur. You may hit too quickly, right from the top, with your hands—and if they have been used at the top, of course, they can't be used again at the bottom—or you may lead so emphatically with your legs and the lower part of your body that your hands and the club are left behind. This causes a flipping action up there. The clubface likely will be left open and you'll hit the ball dead right. . . or worse. Once I went through an extended period of shanking like this, and I couldn't cure it— until I found I was driving my legs so quickly that I was leaving the club at the top.

Feeling leisurely is a thought that works. In my earlier playing days, I developed what felt like a complete hesitation. It was very brief, and I probably never did come to a full stop at the top. So the smoother and slower you can be at the very top of the swing, and then starting down, the better you'll strike the ball.

That smoothness never cost me distance. I hit the ball plenty far. I had no trouble reaching any normal par-5 in two shots. I hit a 2-iron 200 to 210 yards, a 1-iron 220 to 230. They measured my driving in the Chicago Victory Open during the war and I averaged 250 yards. I could even keep up with Snead, and he was a long hitter. I don't think I could have consistently kept up with the likes of Nicklaus and Weiskopf, but I could drive with most of the others on the tour today.

The point is, I was able to get this kind of distance while still concentrating on a smooth swing.

BE FIRM BUT RELAXED AT THE TOP

I never had a lot of wrist action at the top of my swing, although my hands were very high. My wrists were probably fully hinged, although I didn't feel a great deal of cocking action because my left wrist was pretty straight or flat in relation to my forearm. I guess that means I was one of the first to play from a square position at the top. And from there you can't hit the ball very crooked.

By keeping your left wrist straight and firm at the top, and then starting down with the left side of the body turning back toward the ball, your hands will drop inside into hitting position. In my case, I think this method actually forced me to cock my wrists a bit more. You never have to think about a "delayed" hit doing it this way, because the hit will happen naturally. On the other hand, if you allow the left wrist to cup or break inward too much at the top of the swing, you won't be able to hold back the uncocking of your wrists. This action encourages the hit impulse—you'll feel as though your

7. Let the right elbow swing free

Trying to keep the right elbow close to the body on the backswing (B) hinders the maximum upper-body coiling needed to achieve power without relying on the hands and wrists. Instead, keep the right arm relaxed and passive. It moves only as a result of your shoulders turning and your left hand and arm pushing the club back and up. In this relaxed state it will swing free of the body (A) as a result of your shoulder turn.

body has gotten ahead of the swing coming down and you'll be tempted to hit from the top with your hands.

Gary Player is a fine example of a man who gets in excellent position at the top of his backswing. His clubface is in an absolutely square position in relation to his swing plane, and from there he can return it squarely to the ball without independently rotating his hands and forearms. The back of his left hand and wrist form a perfectly straight line. His left arm is straight and his left-hand grip is firmly in control of the club. His magnificent left-arm extension has moved his hands high over his shoulders.

Player's right elbow is pointing toward the ground in a very free position, not tucked in tight against his body. He has kept his head relatively still; his right knee is slightly flexed and his weight is on the inside of his right foot, never swaying to the outside. In achieving this position, he has avoided any reduction of the stretching and coiling of muscles that results from swaying or over-swinging. His whole body is ready to react and uncoil, delivering the clubhead squarely through the ball at the maximum speed possible.

You must do all this and still feel relaxed at the top, because you play best when you feel no pressure starting down. There should be a certain amount of tautness in the left side and back, but not so much that you feel uncomfortable. It's extremely important that you feel able to start the club down leisurely and smoothly.

LET THE RIGHT ELBOW SWING FREE

Back when I started playing golf, the swing featured a "tight" right elbow. On the backswing, the club was swept around the body on a very flat plane. The hips and shoulders swiveled in unison and the right elbow remained in close to your side. In fact, one of the old teaching gimmicks was to have the player tuck a handkerchief under his right armpit and try to keep it there during his swing.

This resulted in a compact swing and gave a player the control he needed to hit straight shots with his whippy, wooden-shafted clubs. But because of that tight right elbow it was also a short swing, which greatly restricted power and distance. To get added yardage with this swing, you had to rely to a great degree on your hands and wrists to

supply the power, usually at the cost of accuracy.

This preoccupation with keeping the right elbow close to the body has lasted to this day. But it is not compatible with the modern golf swing, which depends on a minimum of lower-body turn and a maximum of upper-body coiling to achieve power without relying on the hands and wrists. To make the full shoulder turn that this swing demands, your right arm must be relaxed and free (see illustration #7). Tension in the right arm and shoulder inhibits a full, free turn and reduces your potential for distance.

I've suggested that you address the ball with your right hand and arm relaxed and folded slightly inward to your side. During the backswing, don't concern yourself with your right arm at all, because the right arm should never direct movement. It should stay passive and move only as a result of your shoulders turning and your left hand and arm pushing the club back and up. Because it is relaxed, it will swing free of the body as a result of your shoulder turn.

Jack Nicklaus often has been accused of having a "flying" right elbow. It is not really flying at all; it simply has been pulled away from his side as a result of his big shoulder turn. Jack's elbow remains pointing generally at the ground, in proper position, instead of outward toward the horizon. Yours will, too, if you keep it relaxed and let it respond to the movement of your left side and your shoulders. In this way, your right arm will be free to react to the downward and forward pulling action of the left hand, arm and side during the downswing, and it will come into play at the right time to provide the power you need.

KEEP YOUR ARM SPEED STEADY THROUGHOUT THE SWING

You can't place too much emphasis on smoothness in your swing, but you can overdo the slowness. Many golfers—probably the majority—swing too fast, destroying their rhythm and any chance they might have of timing their swing properly. But many players *do* swing too slowly. I find this especially true with the ladies. A slow, deliberate swing increases the prospect of creating tension, and it certainly prohibits free motion. Moreover, a painfully deliberate backswing often causes, as a reaction, an extremely fast downswing, and this means the sure ruination of good rhythm.

The answer is to swing as most good professionals do—with about the same speed throughout the swing. That speed will vary with the individual and his particular metabolism. It could be slow or fast, but it should always be smooth and rhythmic. Basically, it depends on how much strength you have to control the club going back and starting down. But your guideline should be to keep your arm speed steady in both directions.

TEMPO PRODUCES POWER

Swinging smoothly at the right speed gives you proper tempo. This is vital if you are to get the correctly timed unhinging of your wrists that you need for power, particularly with the long irons and woods. As I've mentioned, the speed of your swing is of little importance as long as it is smooth and unified. Ben Hogan has a reasonably fast backswing. So does Arnold Palmer. But both swings are very smooth.

The average player seems to have trouble making this smooth swing. Even some better players get too anxious to hit the ball. This anxiety is predominant in the long irons, because most players lack confidence in these clubs. And it is with the long irons that a rushed swing is most damaging, because the club-to-ball contact must be so precise.

To help make my swing smoother, I used a counting sequence—one, two, three, four—not a march tempo but slower, for a fox trot. On the count of 1, I took the club away; at 2, I was halfway back; at 3, I was at the top and starting back down; and at 4, I was swinging the club through the ball.

Once a player has developed a smooth rhythm to his swing, he need only make certain that everything moves together as a unit on the backswing. If you don't let the hands and arms speed ahead and get out of step, everything else will follow in good sequence.

Here's an important point about tempo: I don't think a person should go against his natural way of doing things any more than he or she has to. I don't mean you shouldn't try to calm yourself down a bit if you're too high strung or pep yourself up a little if you're too easy-going. But if you carry this to extreme, your swing speed is not going to be natural and your tempo will desert you under pressure.

Earlier, I singled out Gene Littler for his

great tempo, his smooth rhythm. Gene walks and talks that same way. Nicklaus has great rhythm in his powerful swing. His lifestyle also is very solid and deliberate. Julius Boros is another who appears to move pretty calmly through life and matches it with a smooth, almost lazy swing.

If this is not your nature, and your problem is a swing that's too fast and jerky to be effective, there are a couple of things you can do to slow yourself down. First, slow down your breathing. Breathe a little deeper. You'll catch yourself breathing particularly fast during moments of pressure on the course, and you'll have trouble making a good swing if that's happening. Calm down your breathing and you'll calm down your body. That will change your whole way of swinging the club. I know. I was fast and fidgety in my early days, until I learned how to calm myself down this way.

Another good antidote to quickness is to move your feet more slowly during the address and the waggle. Make a deliberate effort to do this, and you'll find it one of the easiest and best ways in the world to slow down your swing.

Most players rush their shots because they're not playing well and they've lost confidence. We're all a little jumpier, a little faster, when we're not confident of what's going to happen. When you're driving an automobile down a straight stretch of highway with no cars in sight, and you're confident you've got the car under control, you can sit there relaxed and steer it with one hand. But once you get in heavy traffic where you don't know exactly what's going to happen, you tighten up. Both hands grip the wheel and you steer the car deliberately instead of just rolling down the road. The same thing happens with your golf swing.

A good example of what poor tempo can do to your swing occurred during Tom Watson's final round in the 1974 U. S. Open. He shot a 79 at the end of 54 holes, after leading the tournament, and finished tied for fifth. I was watching Tom on television during the last round and I covered every shot he hit from the 11th hole on in. It was apparent to me that he was swinging much too quickly, and that as a result he wasn't staying down to the ball or keeping the club on line.

When the round was over, and we had signed off TV, I knew where I could find Watson. He was sitting in the upstairs locker room at Winged Foot. I got him a Coke and sat down next to him. Soon he began to relax and talk about his game. I told him that a lot of great players had gone through just what he had. I explained to him that when he · became tense and tight his swing got too quick and he couldn't stay down to the ball. His head was coming up the minute he made contact and this action was pulling his swing up with it.

Tom has a very fast swing to start with, and he has a very quick waggle. I told him there was nothing wrong with his swing, but that he must tone down his fidgety hand action, smooth it out and let that carry on through his swing. Well, he took my advice and he has gone on to play very well.

Watson still has a fast swing and probably always will. That's because he talks, moves and does everything quickly. But he keeps that swing under control now; it all goes back to the fact that anyone can modify his natural inclinations without making extreme changes.

BALANCE MARKS A GOOD PLAYER

All great players have good balance, which they learn to maintain throughout their swing. To a certain extent, balance is something you're born with, but you certainly can develop a lot of it in your golf swing.

A number of years ago I was doing some panel discussions around the country with the late Horton Smith for the Professional Golfers' Association. During one of these sessions a younger player asked Horton what he felt was the best thing about my golf game. Horton had watched me play all of my tournament life and he said, "I never saw Byron hit a shot on which he lost his balance. Regardless of the terrain, I never once saw him off balance."

That was a great compliment. I'm sure this ability is something I developed by practicing into those Texas winds, because when you're hitting into the wind you *must* maintain your balance. If you're going to hit the ball consistently under those conditions, you can't move at all. And that's generally true with any golf shot.

Balance starts with your setup—the position you take when you stand at the ball (*see illustration #8*). You must have both feet solidly on the ground. If your weight is either too much toward the toes or too much toward the heels, you'll tend

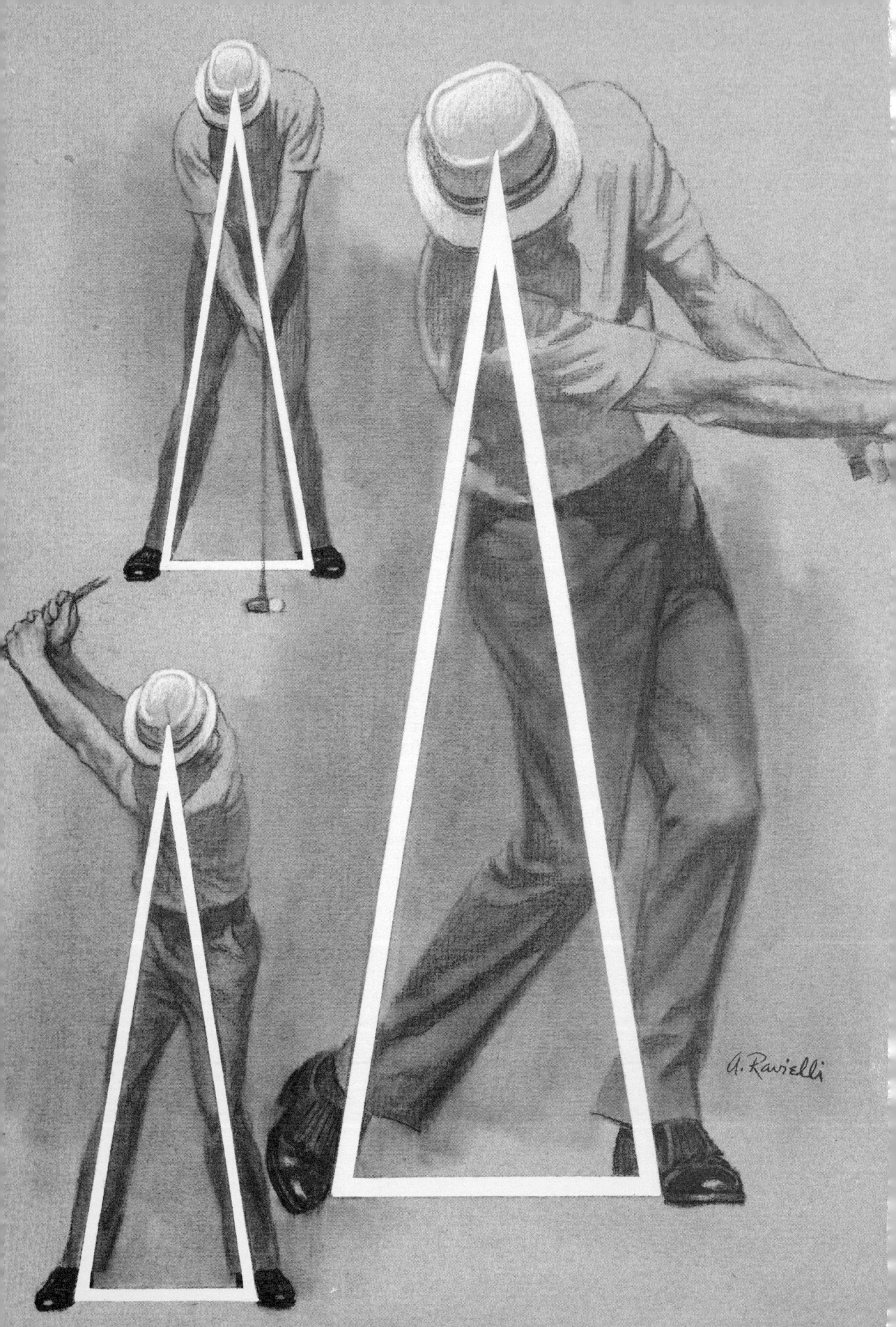

8. A steady head is the key to balance

To stay in balance during the swing, your weight must be properly distributed at address—toward the insides of the feet, not too much toward the heels or the toes, and equally distributed between left and right. After that, the key thought is to keep your head in the same relative position while your body moves freely underneath it on the backswing and downswing. A smooth tempo is vital in maintaining this steady head position and good balance during the swing.

to lose your balance during the swing. Your weight must be toward the insides of your feet, and your knees must be flexed. Your feet must be the proper width apart to maintain balance and still make a good, free turn—about shoulder width for the driver and narrower for the shorter shots where you're not making as big a turn.

You must not stand with too much weight on either the left foot or the right foot, because if you do you'll be forced to make too much of a counter-movement during the swing. You'll try too hard to do this, and the overcompensation that results will cause you to lose your balance.

You must make a proper transfer of your weight—to the right foot on the backswing and to the left on the forward swing. If you do not, you'll have to make all kinds of compensating movements that will pull you off balance. But when you're transferring your weight to the right on the backswing, be sure that you don't get your weight to the outside of your right foot. This will cause you to move your body "off the ball" and force an over-reaction in an effort to get back into position.

Once you've assumed this proper position with the correct weight distribution, the key to maintaining the balance during the swing is to keep your head still.

That brings us to *sway*. Now, when a tree sways, what is moving? The top of the tree, not the trunk. The trunk is stationary. In the golf swing, you want an action that is exactly opposite. You can move considerably underneath your head, and as long as that head stays still you can keep your balance nicely. But once you let that head move, you're going to have to return it to the position it was in originally. That's a difficult thing to do, because now you've disoriented your whole swing and your balance is gone.

You must not, however, try to keep the head *rigid*. If you do that, you create tension that can ruin the freedom of your swing. You must have your head cocked slightly to the right at address so you're looking at the ball out of your left eye—if you look at it out of your right eye, your head will be out of position. After that, you can rotate it slightly counter-clockwise just as you start the swing. A lot of great players play that way: Nicklaus does and Bobby Jones, Walter Hagen and Ben Hogan did, too. I did it some, although not as much as the others. We all tended to tilt or rotate our heads just slightly as we began our backswings. Some players even move their head slightly downward during the forward swing. Nicklaus is an excellent example of this. But all fine players will keep the head in the same relative position throughout the swing, no matter what.

Finally, and I can't state it too strongly, the most vital factor in maintaining balance—whether you're a fast swinger or a slow swinger—is that you swing smoothly. There should be no jerks or jumps or swift takeaways to prevent all parts of the body from moving together in unison. If you move too quickly or before you're ready—on either the backswing or the downswing— then you're going to lose your balance. So keep it smooth and rhythmical.

LEAD THE DOWNSWING WITH A FREE LEFT SIDE

When I began playing, golfers were taught to "hit against a firm left side" on the downswing. That was because we were playing with those whippy wooden shafts. By firming and stiffening the left leg we slowed down the hands and gave the clubhead a chance to catch up.

That sort of action isn't necessary today with our modern, stiffer-shafted clubs. They will straighten themselves by the time the clubhead reaches the ball without your having to slow down the hands. By slowing down your hands today, you'll only sacrifice clubhead speed and distance.

Unfortunately, you still hear that old bromide about the "firm left side." I'd like to lay it to rest for good right now. The good player today keeps his legs slightly flexed at all times. His left leg doesn't straighten until the finish of his swing, and usually not even then. It stays free and sliding toward the target through impact. This means that you are improving your chances for square contact, because you are staying down with the shot. Your clubhead is moving along at ball level for a longer distance in the hitting area. And, of course, by keeping your lower body moving toward the target while your head stays back, your hands aren't slowing down and causing you to lose clubhead speed.

DON'T TRY TO HIT IT

"Accelerate the clubhead into the ball".... "Pour your hands into the shot".... "Give 'er hell at the bottom."

You've often heard those expressions

and others like them, and they sound good. Unfortunately, they don't work. Whenever you consciously try to *hit* the ball on the downswing, to pour on the power in the impact area, you will inevitably do it too early. You will throw the club with your hands or lunge with your shoulders from the top of the swing. This destroys your timing, dissipates clubhead speed and yanks the clubhead off line.

Deliberate clubhead acceleration through the ball is desirable—and obtainable—on short shots and putts. But it's humanly impossible to deliberately accelerate the clubhead into the ball on a full shot. Take a drive, for example: the clubhead has so far to travel, the swing is so long and the buildup of centrifugal force so great that the clubhead approaches impact so fast all you can do is hang on.

I know why players, including some of the good ones, have thought they were hitting at the bottom. As the increase in centrifugal force causes the wrists to unhinge and the clubhead to be "exploded" into the impact area, it *feels* as if the hands are accelerating and hitting. In fact, they are just letting it happen.

The clubhead actually is starting to decelerate at impact. Electronic analysis has shown that. My swing has been clocked many times, and on none of those occasions did I make a swing in which the clubhead accelerated into the ball. My maximum swing speed was clocked at about 167 feet per second, or 114 miles per hour, and I reached that speed just *before* impact. That means I definitely was not pouring on the power with my hands at that stage. The golfers who hit the long ball do so because they are able to keep this deceleration to a minimum.

To do this, turn your shoulders fully on the backswing while keeping a firm grip, an extended left arm and good balance. Then lead your downswing with your feet and legs. Drive them smoothly toward the target, and at the same time swing down with your arms. If you do this without allowing your head to slide forward with your legs, you'll generate much more clubhead speed—and therefore distance—than if you deliberately try to hit the ball.

FREEDOM DOWN BELOW KEEPS THE HEAD STILL

Maintaining your head position is vital during the backswing as well as the downswing. I mentioned earlier a slight

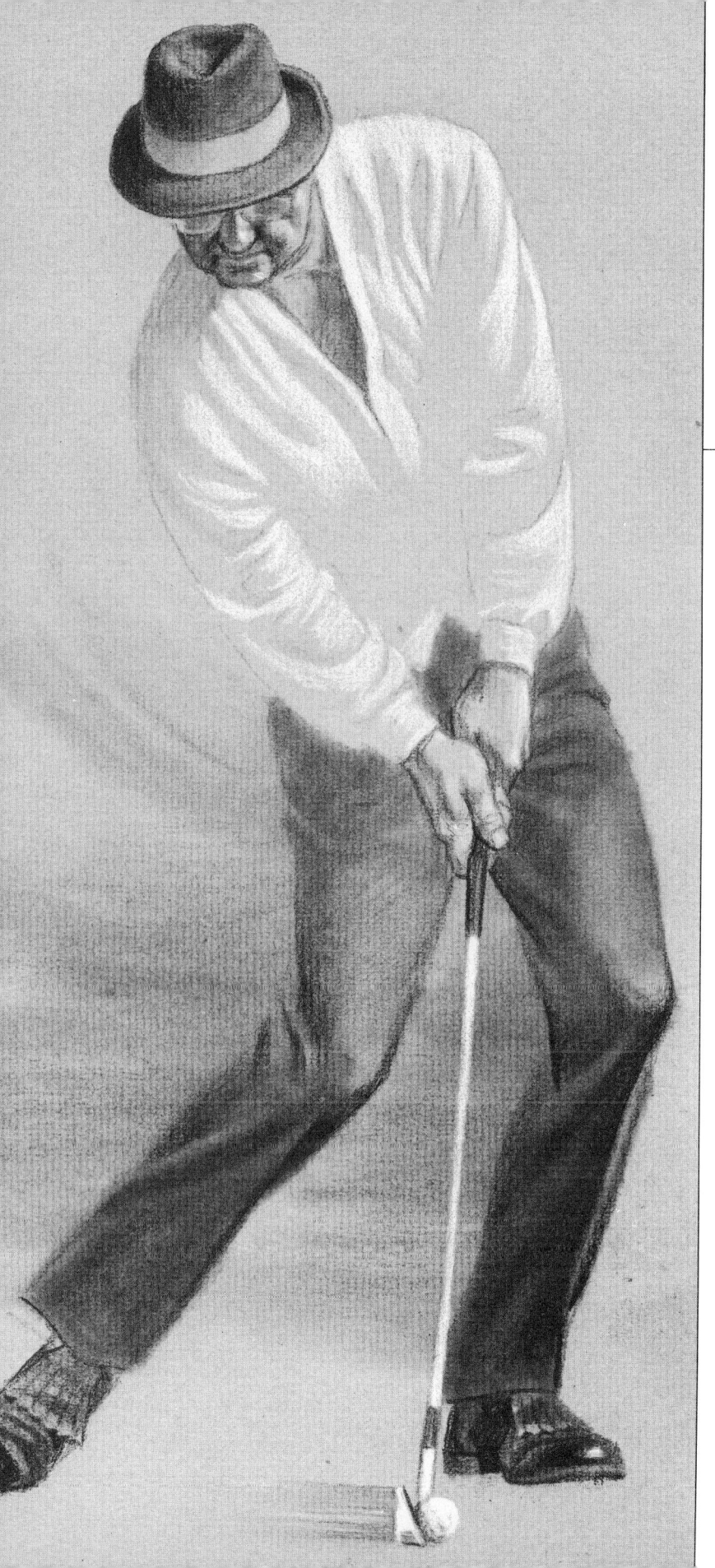

9. Freedom down below keeps the head still

Stiffness in the legs and lower body will cause your head to sway laterally or raise up and down. To maintain the steady head position that is so vital, turn your right side freely out of the way on the backswing and keep your legs flexed and moving freely toward the target on the downswing. This freedom down below allows you to keep your head in position without lessening the power in your shot.

lateral movement of the hips at the start of the backswing but cautioned you not to overdo it. Keep your head in the same position going back; this will allow the right side to keep turning out of the way and let the left side come inward and under. If you let your head move and sway to the right on the backswing, you will block your turn. The right side will stay firm and not move, causing your left side to come out and around, with the left knee moving out toward the ball instead of in toward the right knee. When you start down from the top, that left knee will spin back away from the ball. When it does, you'll get a twisting motion of the shoulders. That's one of the main causes of coming "over the top" of the ball.

Watch Jack Nicklaus some time and see how beautifully he makes the proper turn. With his head steady, his right side moves out of the way. At the top of the swing, his left side is just hanging, ready to move correctly into action when he starts down.

While you must be conscious of keeping your head still in the early stages of building your swing, there's another ingredient required in order to be successful at it: *freedom of body movement (see illustration #9 and also illustration #6, p. 55)*. This is vital if you are to maintain proper head position. Without freedom down below, your swing will be too stiff and something must give. Most often it's the head that moves out of position. You rarely see a good player with this problem, because good golfers move freely with their legs to get maximum power, and this frees the swing to keep the head in position.

Stiff-legged action will cause your head to sway laterally. Also, improper use of your legs will cause the head to lower and raise. If, during your backswing, you point your left knee straight out and increase its flex instead of letting it roll inward toward the right, it will tend to lower your head. This usually is followed by a lifting on the downswing as your left knee stiffens.

SWING OUT FROM UNDER YOUR HEAD

I can't emphasize too much the fact that your lower body must lead the downswing while your head remains relatively still. You must create the sensation of swinging past your chin, of keeping your head back while your hips and legs swing past it toward the target. The best way I can describe the feeling is that *you swing completely out from under your head*. Your body moves clear past the point of your chin and your arms swing into the follow-through before your head moves.

STAY DOWN AND THROUGH

After a lifetime of watching golf—as a player, television commentator and observer who still goes to an average of 20 tournaments a year—I've come to the conclusion that one of the big problems faced by the lesser player, and even some of those on tour, is that he does not stay *down and through* the ball long enough.

I've explained earlier (in Chapter 3, p. 54) about staying down and through. What exactly does that mean? The average player thinks it refers only to keeping his head still, not looking up. This is necessary, but it's not what I'm talking about.

At the moment of impact most players come up too quickly with the body and head, following the turn of the left shoulder. They end up looking right at the ball in an upright position. They might hit some shots straight, but when the pressure is on they'll exaggerate this straightening of the left side. This can cause any number of errors, such as pulling the ball to the left or hitting it thin.

The better player, on the other hand, stays down through the hitting area much longer with his body by keeping his knees flexed, his left side leading and his head back (*see illustration* #10). The right side comes down and under instead of up and around, and the clubhead trajectory is as low as possible, following the ball as it goes through the shot. An iron, especially, is still traveling on a downward arc as it makes contact with the ball. Because the ball is played slightly forward in your stance for a driver shot, the club will be traveling on a more level path or even slightly on the upswing at impact. The player who swings this way will hit the ball more solidly and his shots will be straighter.

That little dip they talked about in my swing happened because my knees were staying flexed and moving laterally farther than usual. I might not recommend that much leg action for everybody, but it had its advantages for me. I once went to Purdue University, where they took some pictures of me and four other leading players of the time. Those pictures proved that my club was on line longer and lower going back and through than any of the others. I think that's another reason why my shots had less curvature to them.

10. Stay down and through
Staying down to the ball means keeping the body, rather than just the head, down through the hitting area. To do this, keep the knees flexed, the left side leading and the head back during impact and beyond. The right side will come down and under instead of up and around on the forward swing, and the clubhead trajectory should remain as shallow as possible through the shot. Your club will stay longer on the target line and your shots will be straighter.

One of the great players who swung much the same way I'm describing was Cary Middlecoff, twice U. S. Open champion and once a Masters champion. Cary had a strongly developed leg action and, by keeping his head in the right position, he allowed the hands and club to follow straight through and keep the ball on line.

Tony Lema once told me that he had watched me practice for so long that he incorporated that move with the legs into his own swing, and he did look very much like me in the hitting area.

Among the modern players, Tom Watson and Tom Weiskopf are excellent examples of players who never really do straighten up throughout the swing. Their knees are still well flexed at the finish.

Every player should try to develop this motion, in which the left side is flexed and the head kept back as you swing through the shot. Don't look after the ball until the right shoulder has come to its lower position in the impact area. When that happens, the head will come up naturally.

CHAPTER 5: SPECIAL THOUGHTS TO DEVELOP POWER AND CONSISTENCY

In chapters 3 and 4, you learned about the fundamental thoughts that apply to your basic swing motion. What follows is a collection of more specific ideas that you can use to achieve the primary purpose of the swing—that is, to strike the ball consistently with power and control with all the clubs.

Hang on with the left hand for consistency: You control the club on the downswing with the hand that took it back. I don't think anybody who knows much about golf would argue with that statement. I used to hear people—including some good players—say that the club slipped in their left hand. I know Bob Jones said he let loose of the club with his left hand at the top of his swing, and perhaps this was one reason why Bob was inconsistent at times. Well, I don't ever remember losing the club in my left hand once in my entire life.

Visualize your target: One of the most important—and often overlooked—factors in making a good golf swing is visualizing your target beforehand. In golf, the ball is not your target, although most people seem to think it is. The spot where you want your ball to finish is the target, and by being aware of that spot, you give your swing direction.

Some players pick a spot close by—maybe three or four feet away but in line with their eventual target—and they swing toward that. Jack Nicklaus does it this way and it's obviously a good technique. I always picked a target farther away. If I wasn't shooting at the green or didn't have the pin to go for, I'd line up on a bunker or a tree, the chimney of a faraway house or just a spot on the fairway. That became the line on which I wanted the ball to travel. I would then simply take the club straight back along that line, with the target still in my mind's eye, and try to return it directly toward that target.

Try it for yourself. I think you'll be amazed at how much straighter you hit your shots.

If you swing harder, stand closer: Here's a tip when you need more distance on a particular shot and have to swing harder. Stand a little bit closer to the ball at address, because if you swing harder you're inclined to push more with your feet and legs and raise up a bit. If you didn't move closer at address, you'd hit the ball too thin.

After moving in closer to the ball, take the club back slower and longer. This gives you a bigger arc and generates more clubhead speed. At the same time, this longer arc lessens any inclination you might have to hit too hard and too soon with your hands.

On taking divots and getting backspin: The good player will not take a large divot, especially from a normal lie. He'll take a thin slice of turf, but he won't dig out a big chunk.

If you're gouging a divot, you should check to see if you're moving on the ball too much—swaying too far onto the left side before you hit it, or using the right side too early in the downswing. Your iron clubhead should be traveling slightly downward when it contacts the ball, but the more it approaches a level path, the better your swing and your shot will be.

Remember, the amount of backspin you get does not depend on the size of your divot. Backspin comes simply from the ball climbing up the clubface at impact, not from the clubface pinching it against the turf. So slice—don't dig— your divots.

Woods vs. irons: Most players can use fairway woods better than long irons. The wood has a bigger, more solid-looking head, which gives the higher handicappers more confidence. They get it in their heads that they have to force shots with the thin-bladed long irons, so they try to hit it too hard and consequently don't play as well. That's why I would advise the casual player to use the fairway woods, even going so far as to add a 6- and 7-wood to his set. He'll have more success than he would with the long irons and he'll enjoy the game more.

But if you are sincere about improving your game, you should practice your long irons and develop confidence and skill with them. By learning to use them properly, you can control them better than you can the fairway woods and they will—they must—become important weapons in your arsenal.

The full swing is the same with all clubs: I don't feel the iron swing is basically any different than the swing you use with a wood. It changes naturally because an iron is not as long as a wood (your driver is 42 or 43 inches long; your 2-iron only 38½ or 39). So you're three

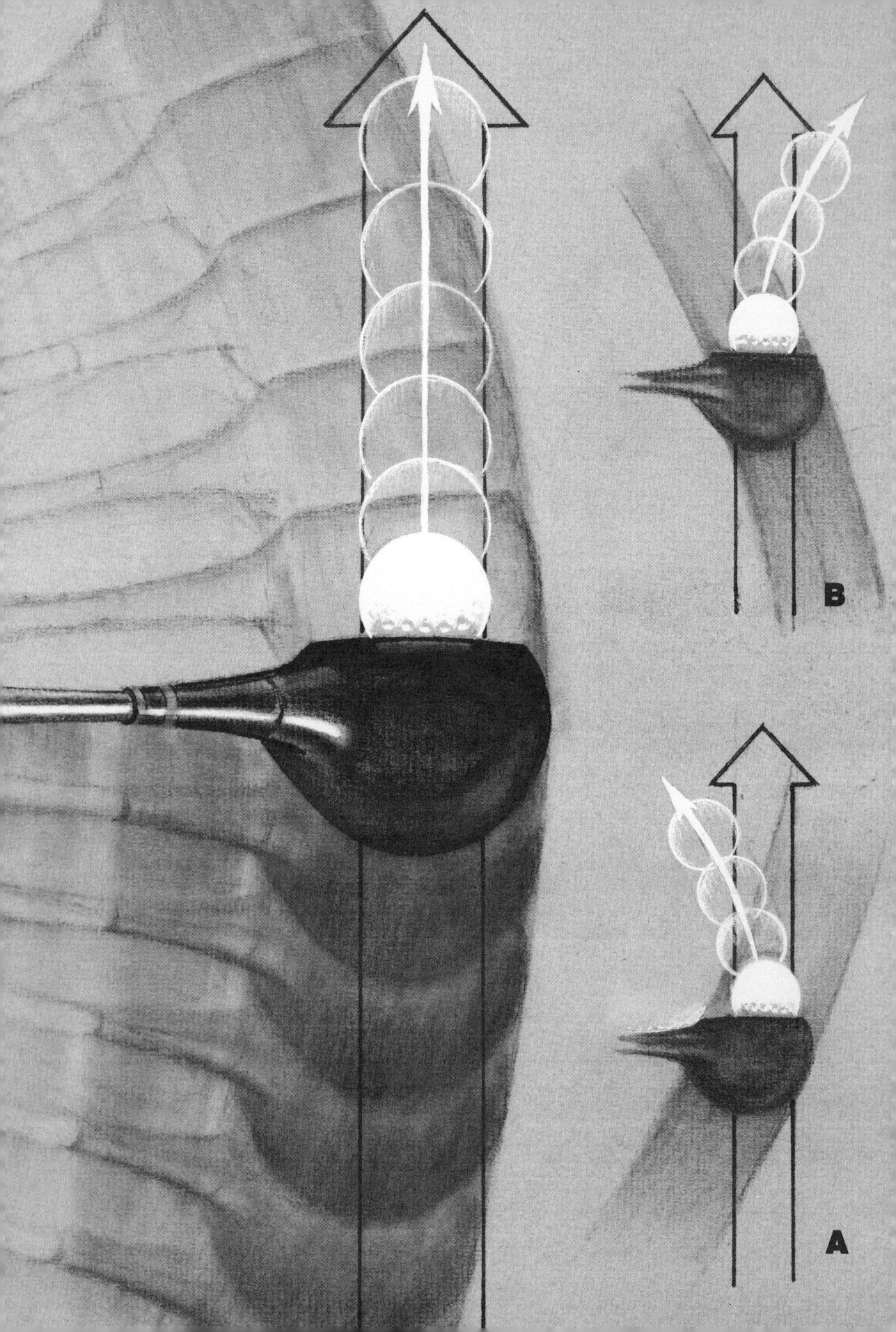

11. Ideal clubhead path is from inside to along the line

The ideal clubhead path is from inside to along the line at impact. After the ball is struck, the clubhead naturally swings back quickly inside the target line. This ensures the straightest shot. If the club is traveling from inside to outside during impact, the ball will hook, assuming the clubface is square to the target (A). If the club comes from outside to inside the line with a square face, the result will be a slice (B).

inches closer to the ball with an iron, which means you're naturally going to swing a little more upright, hitting more down on the shot and taking some turf instead of sweeping it as you do the wood. As the irons get shorter and more lofted, of course, you will swing even more upright. But you should not consciously try to make any modifications.

One fault that a lot of players share is standing too far away from the ball with an iron. Instead of standing closer as they should, they bend over more than they do with a fairway wood, and this distorts their swing pattern. So be sure to assume your normal address posture and let your swing plane take care of itself.

The clubhead travels from inside to along the line: The ideal clubhead path during your swing is from inside the target line to along that line during impact (*see illustration #11*). After impact, the club swings back quickly inside the line as a result of the natural turning of your hips and shoulders.

If you slice, one likely cause is that your clubface is moving across the target line from outside to inside. This means the clubface is striking the ball a glancing blow and imparting the clockwise spin that causes a slice.

Since this problem is so prevalent, teachers for years have advocated that slicers try to swing the clubhead from inside to outside the target line in an effort to offset their normal outside-to-inside pattern. There is some logic to this, because it might be necessary to over-correct in order to learn how a radical new swing feels.

But you must realize that the inside-to-outside swing path is not ideal. Such a path will never result in sending the ball straight to the target. A swing path that comes from inside to along the target line at impact *will* result in straight shots.

Hit the back of the ball: I've heard golfers say they try to hit their tee shots with overspin to get more distance. I'm sure you've heard it said that a hooked shot, or one that draws from right to left, has overspin and so will roll farther when it lands.

This kind of thinking leads to all sorts of disasters. A player who operates with this philosophy might try to roll his clubface counterclockwise during impact to produce the hookspin that is supposed to make the ball go farther. All

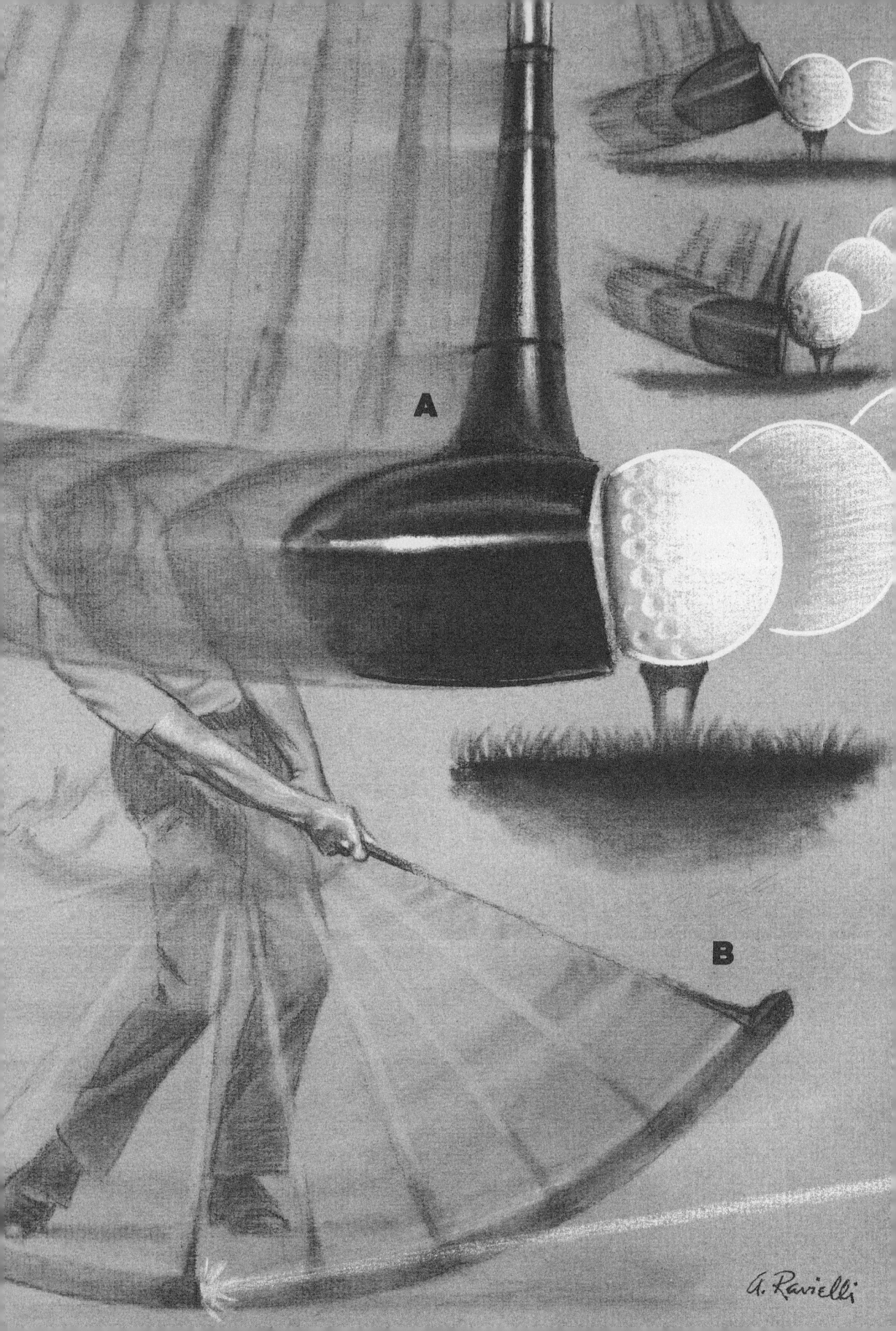

12A. Strike the back of the ball
To achieve the proper trajectory on your shots, neither too high nor too low, envision your clubhead moving squarely into the back of the ball on as shallow an arc as possible. Do not try to put overspin on the ball by swinging up, and be careful not to strike too much of a descending blow. This only pops the ball up.

12B. The 'hit' is from ball on through
The worst thing you can do is hit at the ball. Rather, think of contact as being from the ball on through. As you come into the impact area you should feel that your swing is gaining momentum and everything is speeding from the ball on through toward the target. You should actually feel the clubhead being thrown toward the target.

---

that he will accomplish is to reduce the chances of bringing the clubface squarely into the ball at impact, or increase the chances of striking the ball a glancing blow—rather than a solid one (see illustration #12A). This inevitably leads to a premature releasing of the hands, thus reducing clubhead speed. Or he might try to tee the ball higher and hit it with an upward stroke. Either he will hit behind the ball or top it—and that, incidentally, is the *only* way you can put overspin on a shot.

The truth of the matter is, scientific tests have proven time and again that it is impossible to strike the ball squarely and still impart overspin to it. It always will leave the clubface with backspin. That backspin, in fact, is what keeps the ball airborne—so we don't want to avoid it, we want to encourage it. We are trying to achieve the proper trajectory on our shots, neither too high nor too low.

The best way to do this is to swing the clubhead squarely into the back of the ball. If the clubhead is moving at ball level and squarely along the target line at impact, you will get the maximum distance-producing force. So forget about trying to apply overspin and simply hit the back of the ball with the swing method I've already described.

Hit from the ball on through:
One of the most important things to realize about the golf swing is that the hit—and I use that term advisedly—is not *to* the golf ball but *from the ball on through*. You should feel yourself moving smoothly in the early part of the downswing. Then, as you come into the hitting area, everything just flies. Your swing gains momentum and you feel everything—feet, legs, hips, left shoulder, arms and hands—speed from the ball on through (see illustration #12B). You feel as if the clubhead is being thrown toward the hole.

This actually happens in a good swing—but don't *try* to make it happen. You must instead program this image in your mind before you make the shot, then just let it happen. Don't try to hit it; instead, develop the feeling that the ball is going to go a long way without your really trying. And sure enough, it will. It also will go very straight if you let your swing flow through the ball with the left side in control, without making any conscious effort to steer the shot.

Hook from an open face: Back in the mid-1950s, I worked with Harvie Ward, who then was probably the best amateur player in the world, having won the U. S. Amateur and the British Amateur back-to-back. The only thing I taught him was how to maneuver the ball. He could go through some contortions and get the ball to hook, but he really didn't have any idea how it was done. When I showed him how to hook the ball from an open clubface, he had no more problems. I can still hear him remark, "I never knew the game could be so simple!"

Ideally, when the clubface makes contact with the ball, it will be square to the intended target line. For the good player, though, the clubhead will be coming from inside the target line, and because of this the heel of the club will be leading the toe. But the arc of the swing and the release of the wrists and hands through impact will cause the toe to catch up. In effect, it is passing the heel.

In this context, the longer you can keep the toe from passing the heel, the straighter you're going to hit the ball. That's why a full extension of the left side and left arm going through the ball is so important. If that left side and arm fold up, the hands are going to turn over too quickly, the toe is going to pass the heel too soon and you're going to hook the ball too much.

The interesting thing about this concept is that the better player does indeed hook the ball from an open clubface position at address. I'm talking about the true hook or draw, the ball that starts out to the right of the target and moves back left onto the target. With the proper swing, the club is traveling from inside to down the target line. The clubface is slightly open or pointed to the right at impact, which means the ball will start in that direction. Because the natural release of the hands is closing the face, or making the toe pass the heel, hookspin will be imparted and the ball will draw back on target. This natural release is further aided by the player's instinctive knowledge that he must get that open face closed up, so he will rotate his arms more in a counter-clockwise fashion. This is called an offensive blow, as opposed to the blocked shot, in which the player subconsciously keeps the clubface from closing and leaves the ball sailing out to the right.

I won't say you can't hit a wild slice from an open clubface, or a smothered hook from one that is closed, but if you make a proper swing and let your instincts take over, you'll find that what I say is true.

You must repeat your swing to score well: The one thing about my career that has pleased me more than anything is the consistency with which I played. I finished in the money 113 consecutive times when we had only 15 or 20 prizes. And the most important thing I've learned about maintaining consistency is this: *you must develop a swing you can repeat every time*.

The golfers who don't score well are those who don't know what they're going to do when they walk up to a shot—whether they're going to pull it, slice it, top it, hook it or what. Everybody misses golf shots, but the player who scores well is the one who can repeat his swing and hit the same kind of shot most of the time.

I know people with peculiar swings, but because they swing exactly the same way every time, they can score. Miller Barber doesn't exactly have a picture-book swing. He loops his backswing and his hands appear to be way out of position. But because he gets everything going the right way on the downswing, and because he does it the same way with every swing, he has become a very successful professional player.

If you know where the shot is going every time, regardless of whether you're slicing the ball or hooking it, you can play. If you don't know where the shot is going, you'll be in trouble every time.

Ben Hogan used to hook the ball terribly, but I once saw him win a tournament in San Francisco even though he was hooking badly, because he hooked it the same amount each time. He knew how much it was going to hook every time he hit it. The net result was the same as if he'd hit it straight—the ball wound up precisely where he expected it to.

That's an extreme case, and Ben had to learn to hit the ball straight—after all, sometimes there are trees in your way and you can't hook the ball—but his example makes my point. The good players practice to develop a swing that's repeatable, so when they get out there they don't have to think about how they're going to swing and where the ball is going. They're only thinking about where the ball is going to wind up, and what they've got to do to play that particular round of golf and make a good score. They know what they have to do to put the ball where they want it; therefore, they can concentrate on scoring rather than worrying about whether they're going to hook the ball or slice it on every shot.

In the next chapter, I've put together a collection of my ideas on how to improve those all-important short shots around and on the greens, as well as the shots that get you out of trouble. With knowledge and competence in these areas, you can use your solid swing to put lower numbers on the scorecard. I guarantee it.

CHAPTER 6:
NEW TECHNIQUES TO MODERNIZE YOUR OLD SHORT GAME

Because most amateurs miss a lot of greens, they must depend on chip shots, pitches and putts to save par. You really can't place too much importance on these shots—it's the one area of the game where players of all types have a chance to excel. Size and strength are not factors in these stroke-saving shots.

PUTTING

Let's start with the putt, the most important of all these shots because it's the one that gets the ball into the hole. I wish now that I had worked at my putting game more than I did in the early days. The boys today really practice it and this helps tremendously in lowering their scores.

Putting is such an individual thing that nobody can set down absolute rules for doing it. The minute I say there is only one way to putt, somebody will point to Bobby Locke, who seems to violate all the principles. He looks like he hooks every putt. Yet he might have been the best putter anybody ever saw.

In my opinion, there are no fundamental truths that tell you to hold a putter just so or to stand a certain way. Beyond that, however, there are certain things that all good putters do, especially the modern-day players. We had some wonderful putters in my time—Horton Smith, Johnny Revolta, Jimmy Demaret, Lloyd Mangrum and Jackie Burke, to name a few—but as a group the modern players are much better. In my day and time, the players had a more wristy style. They didn't move much except the putter, the hands and the wrists. Today, the putting stroke is more of a solid unit, and it's a better way.

That "better way" includes a number of things that all good putters have in common. For example, they keep their bodies still. Arnold Palmer, one of the greatest in his prime, locks his knees together so he can keep his body still. Good putters also keep their heads still, even after the putter has struck the ball.

Keeping the blade square is something else all good putters do. In fact, it is probably the most important lesson you'll ever learn about putting. The secret is: you must never let the left wrist break down—never let the putterhead pass the hands. If you do, the face of the club will open or close, and you will cut or pull the putt.

Dutch Harrison, who was a wonderful putter, once helped me when I was having trouble. He said, "Byron, the one

13A. Putterhead never passes the left hand
A good putter keeps his body still and the blade square by never allowing his left wrist to break down. The putterhead never passes the left hand throughout the stroke. The putter is not picked up on the backswing but is swung back low, although it should swing up naturally as the stroke gets longer.

13B. Position your eyes over target line
The two important ingredients in a good putting stance are: 1) Bend over far enough so that your arms hang freely with some flex at the elbows and (2) keep your eyes directly over the target line.

thing you should never do when you're coming through the ball is allow the angle of that left wrist to change. The arm and hand and putter have to go through in one piece. If that doesn't happen, you're never going to putt well."

I know that Billy Casper, who is one of the great modern putters, uses a wrist stroke. But he keeps his left hand and wrist firm. He taps the ball with his right hand and the club stops almost at the ball. It's like driving a tack. Because Billy never lets the left wrist break down, he hits the ball with the blade square every time; despite his wrist stroke he maintains the same principle I've referred to above.

Another putting secret: you must not pick the club up going back or through the putt. It should stay low to the line on short putts, because this helps you strike the putt solidly. Remember, I told you to keep the club low going back and through on the full shot. Well, putting is just a shortened version of the full shot.

Lloyd Mangrum, who was absolutely one of the best putters I ever saw, said he actually felt his putter brush the grass as he putted. Jackie Burke, a great touch putter who could roll the ball so well he once went 90 holes at the Masters without three-putting, said he felt the same thing.

Notice, I said the putter stays low on short putts. You should make no attempt to keep it close to the ground on longer putts. If you do, you'll pull yourself out of position. Just let the club swing up naturally. At that point, it will even swing inside the line a little, the amount depending on the length of the putt. The blade will also appear to open, but this is just because of your natural swing arc. If you are making no manipulations with your hands, the blade will be square when it returns to the ball.

The putting stance: In my experience, most good putters follow two key principles in their stance. One is that they bend over enough to have some flex or bend at the elbows (*see illustration #13A*). They're not necessarily sticking way out; they're just hanging in a free position. This allows them to move more easily from the shoulders, with sort of a plunger effect. If your arms are too straight, it is difficult to swing them without causing body movement.

Second, the eyes are always over the target line (*See illustration #13B*). Some players bend over considerably, others

stand straighter. Some have wide stances, others narrow. Some have their knees locked, their toes turned in. But one thing they all have in common is that their eyes are over the line. Sometimes the eyes are back of the ball. Jack Nicklaus, the greatest pressure putter on the tour today, uses that technique. But his eyes are always over the line. This position makes it much easier to see the path to the cup. If your eyes are outside or inside the line, you're going to get a distorted view of your target.

Having the eyes over the line also means that you're not going to be reaching for the ball. This allows you to take the blade back and forth on a straighter line.

I think the most consistent putters over the years have stood with their weight evenly distributed between left and right and the balls and heels of their feet. They get anchored solidly. That goes along with developing a position that's comfortable for you. If you're not comfortable, you're not going to be able to stay there long.

The ball is positioned somewhere between the center of your stance and your left toe. You never see it played back of center or ahead of the left foot anymore, because the good putters have learned that the blade can't be kept on line at those points.

I wouldn't be dogmatic about what initiates the backswing. It looks to me like the finest putters practically all swing from the shoulders. But I've watched some who appear to start it with the hands, while other players have indicated to me that they *feel* like they do it that way. The basic thing to remember is that it should be a one-piece action, with everything starting simultaneously. I think one of the problems when somebody is putting badly is that the hands start a little earlier than the movement of the shoulders.

Whichever method you use to start the backswing, make sure you start it rhythmically and keep it that way. There should be no jerks or exaggerated pauses, just as in the full swing. Again, rhythm is one of the important attributes you can incorporate into your putting stroke.

The putting grip: I have no strong feelings about the kind of putting grip you should use. Most players employ the reverse overlap, in which the forefinger of the left hand is laid across the last two or three fingers of the right. But some use the normal overlapping grip. My own particular grip was a combination of these two styles. I overlapped the little finger of the right hand over the middle finger of the left, with that left forefinger still lying across the right-hand fingers. The reason I like it is that it puts three fingers of each hand on the club. It gets the hands closer together and helps keep the back of the left hand and left wrist firmer.

Whatever style of grip you use, the important thing is to place the hands in position so they can move back and forth in the stroke without causing the putter blade to open and close. Most players do this by placing the hands in a position on the club in which the palms more or less face each other.

Some good putters hold a club firmly. Others, who are more "touch" putters, hold it a lot more lightly. The criterion here is that you don't hold it so tightly that you tense your muscles and interfere with a relaxed stroke, nor so lightly that you allow too much looseness in the wrists, causing the putterhead to pass the hands.

If you asked most great putters, they'd tell you that they grip the club a little firmer with their left hands. Doing that consistently will prevent the left wrist from breaking down and the clubhead from passing the hands.

Nicklaus says he putts with his right hand, and I'll agree that the right hand can be important for many putters. It is, after all, the hand in which you have more feel and sensitivity (if you're a right-handed person, of course). But watch Nicklaus whenever he's urging a putt toward the hole. The putter is in his left hand and his right hand is completely away from it. Back in the days when Arnold Palmer was such a fine putter, he would practically chase the ball to the hole with the putter in his left hand. That certainly indicates which hand is dominant when it comes to putting-grip pressure.

Roll the ball to the hole: Speed also is very important in putting. No matter how well you hit the ball, if you haven't done so at the proper speed, you're not going to make the putt, regardless of how accurately you started it on line.

A piece of bad advice that probably has added more strokes to more golfers' scores than any other is, "Never up,

14. Roll your putts to the hole

On longer putts, think only of rolling the ball to the hole. By consciously trying to make the ball get to or past the hole, you're likely to hit the ball so hard that it has no chance to go in—even if it hits the hole—and will probably end up several feet past. A ball that is dying around the hole has a much better chance to fall in on any side. By not trying to make the putt, you take pressure off yourself and will probably make a better stroke. Practice by rolling a ball out on the green, then roll putts to that ball rather than to a hole.

never in." Obviously, if the ball doesn't get to the hole it has no chance to fall in. But when we think consciously of getting the ball past the hole, we tend to exaggerate—and that's just what happens. We knock it four or five feet past the hole. I've seen people do that and say, "Well, I gave it a chance." They gave it no chance at all. The ball wouldn't have gone in if it had hit the hole dead center! Stroking a putt that firmly also cuts down on the amount of break you can expect on a sidehill putt. So if you've played for the normal break, you'll miss the cup on the high side every time. Striking the ball harder than normal also encourages pushing or pulling the putt.

Instead of "giving it a chance," or trying to make the putt from 20 to 30 feet or more, think about *rolling the ball to the hole* (see illustration #14). Try to make it die right at the hole. This gives you two advantages over the charger: if a dying putt catches any part of the hole, it will fall in; and if it does miss, you won't have a knee-knocker coming back.

I've seen players finish a round of 68, 69 or 70 who are absolutely fatigued, because they've left themselves long second putts all day long. Another player may not have scored any better, but he'll come in relaxed and fresh, because he has rolled the ball close to the hole every time and has made his score with much more ease (and you'll be surprised at how many of those lag putts actually do fall in). If you have to be careful with every second putt, the mental strain eventually will catch up with you by the end of the tournament or even the last few holes of the round.

To develop a touch for the right speed, you must practice, of course. Roll a ball out on the practice green about 30 feet, or whatever length you want to practice, then putt several balls to that ball instead of the hole (see illustration #14). This relieves you of the anxiety of trying to make the putt and lets you see how much your distances vary. Go to another part of the green and do the same thing, and be sure to practice both uphill and downhill putts. Eventually, you will develop a feel for the different distances and know how firmly you must stroke each putt.

Some players—Frank Beard, for example—will try to let the ball die into the hole on all putts, long or short. But I feel that on the shorter putts, up to four feet or so, you should try to strike the ball firmly enough so that it goes into the hole with some momentum. Unless the greens are extremely fast, or you're putting sharply downhill, you should feel that the ball is almost hitting the back of the hole. This makes it a lot easier to maintain your line. I was never renowned as a great putter, but I was always good on short putts because I was firm with them.

If you really want to improve your putting stroke, don't practice long putts (except for the purpose I've already mentioned). Do the putts you should be holing in the two to six-foot range and teach yourself to *make* putts. Don't practice a real difficult putt, because that will destroy your confidence. Subconsciously, you'll begin to feel you can't make a putt.

I've watched a lot of the great putters when they have fallen into an infrequent slump. They'll get out on the practice green, find a level spot two or three feet from the hole, and just make it, make it, make it.

Here's a clue that will make this kind of practice effective. If you're putting well from two or three feet, the ball will roll right into the center of the hole every time. If you're putting badly, the ball will be catching the left and right edges.

Sure, it might be going in, but you know in your heart that if it's not going in dead center at that distance, it will certainly miss the cup from another six or seven feet away.

From that shorter distance, then, it's easier to regain the feeling of keeping the blade square, keeping it going back and through along the line, and getting the ball going into the center of the cup. Stroke enough of those putts until you develop the confidence that you're rolling the ball correctly. Then start moving back a little farther.

Here's another practice device that will help you: push the ball into the practice green with your hand about two or two and a half feet from the hole, making a slight indentation. Next, roll the ball toward the hole with your hand, pressing down hard so you make a little bit of a groove. Then stand there and putt the ball out of that indentation and along the groove until you get tired of seeing it go in the hole. If you're hitting it correctly, keeping the blade low and square and not picking it up or hitting across the ball, it will go in every time. It's a great confidence-building exercise, and confidence is what putting is really all about.

Reading the greens: Another major putting problem for most players is reading the greens properly. To be honest, judging the amount of break on a slope can come only from practice and experience. But I will give you a thought which I think can help. The problem that most poor putters have is not adjusting to the line of the putt. When they take their position to putt, they line up to the hole, then try to adjust the putter blade to the line on which they want to roll the ball.

Don't do that. Pick out the line along which you want to hit the ball, take your position square to that line and roll the ball along that line, disregarding the hole.

Even when a player lines up properly on a breaking putt, either to the right or left, he will subconsciously try to *make* the putt break the way he wants it to. He may think he's starting the ball along the proper line, but he'll instinctively shove it toward the hole at the same time, which means he'll miss the putt below the hole every time.

Instead, *believe* in the line you pick and let the putter swing along that line. If you've chosen the correct line, the ball will break into the cup. You're certainly not going to make the putt any other way.

Incidentally, I dislike spot putting, which is the practice of picking out a spot at which to aim. I find that whenever I try this I instinctively make the ball die at the spot instead of in the cup. I prefer to visualize a line, either straight or curved, depending on the slope and grain, that runs all the way from ball to cup. Try this method and trust yourself to hit the ball along that line and I think you'll have more success.

Trusting yourself and your stroke is, of course, the main key to success in putting. You must think positively. Keep all thoughts of missing the putt out of your mind. The best way to do this in my opinion is simply to concentrate on what you have to do to *make* the putt—the way you want to roll the ball, the line on which it will travel and the mechanics you must use to send it there. Do this before you step up to putt. Once these positive thoughts are firmly implanted in your mind, let your stroke simply react to the target as naturally and smoothly as you can.

CHIPPING AND PITCHING

It's really not difficult to get the ball close to the hole from just off the green. A lot of

15A. De-loft club for crisper chips
In chipping, hood or de-loft the club by moving your hands forward at address. Be sure the blade is kept square to the intended line. This de-lofting motion helps you strike the ball before you clip the grass.

15B. Chip with freedom in your legs
The most important thing in the chip or short pitch shot is to execute it with freedom in your legs. Feel a little rocking motion, with a very slight transfer of weight in your legs from left to right and back to left, your legs moving smoothly but slightly toward the target on the forward swing. The legs should lead just as in a full shot, but on a smaller, quieter scale.

people I used to play against would rather have seen me on the green with a long putt than a short chip, because I used to hole so many from off the edge. I've holed as many as two or three chip shots in a round. Whether you reach that level of skill depends simply on how hard you want to work at it.

Too many players are not proficient around the greens because, for one thing, they don't practice these shots. They prefer instead to stand on the range and whack tee shots when they practice. Secondly, they simply don't understand the technique of chipping and pitching. I can't help you with your practice. You'll have to do that yourself. But I can give you some thoughts that will help you understand how these valuable little shots are made.

The most important thing I can tell you about these shots—and I talk about it first because I want to emphasize it—is that *you must have freedom in the legs* to execute them successfully. Most players try to do it too much with the hands. As a result, the left side doesn't stay in a leading position, the right hand takes over, and you either top the shot or hit behind it. "Chili-dip it," as they say.

Once that starts to happen, the player begins to compound the error. Instead of loosening up so he can move more with the lower body and achieve good timing, he gets tense and is afraid to move at all. That just makes things worse.

Now, understand that I'm not talking about a lot of movement—and none at all in the head. You must keep your head perfectly still on these delicate little shots. With the legs, however, you should feel a very slight transfer of weight from the left to the right and back to the left again—just a little bitty rocking motion. Your legs move smoothly, if slightly, toward the target as you come through. In other words, they're leading the way and generating the force, just as in the full shot, but on a much smaller and quieter scale (*see illustration #15B*).

That action is particularly effective if you do have trouble with chili-dipping a lot. As a cure, feel as if you're striking the shot only with your legs—as if you've eliminated your hands entirely. For a while, you'll have the sensation that you're going to hit the ball too hard, but once your hand action has quieted down you'll quickly develop a feel for the shot.

In chipping, you want the ball to be rolling as long as possible, yet you must land it on the green. If you land the ball

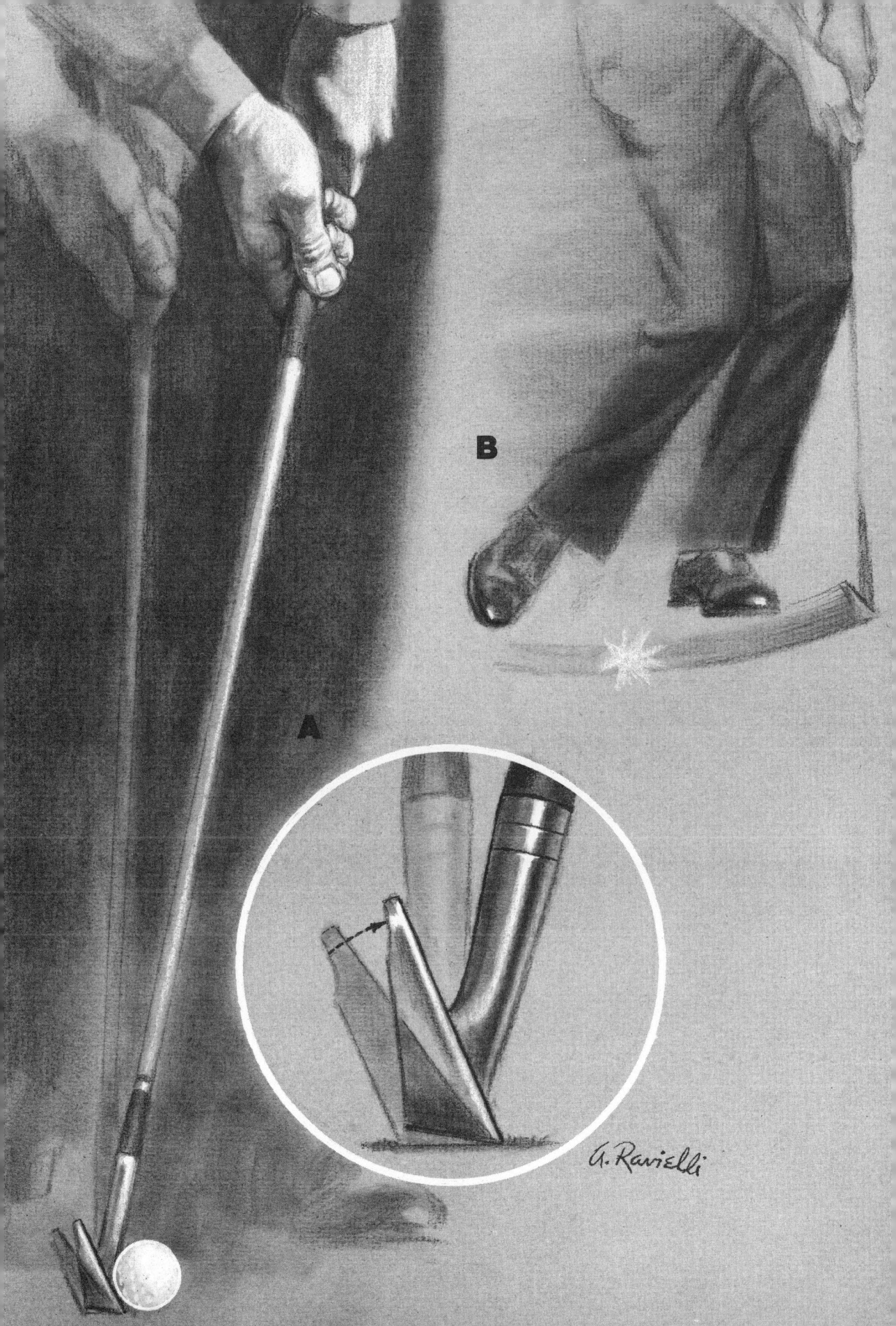

on the fringe, you won't get as true an action as if it landed on the putting surface. So select your club accordingly. If the pin is way across the green from you, you might want to chip with a straighter-faced club—a 4- or 5-iron. If it's close and you don't have much green to work with, perhaps an 8-iron or even a pitching wedge is the best club.

Whatever club you choose, you should hood (or de-loft) it a bit by moving your hands forward at address, taking care to keep the blade square to your intended line (*see illustration #15A*). You want to make sure you strike the ball before you clip the grass, and that's easier to do if the face is hooded slightly. It's something all good chippers do.

I recommend that you weaken your left hand on the club—turn it to the left or counterclockwise—so that your palms are in a facing position. This keeps the back of your hand and the clubface always facing the target. It further insures that the left hand won't collapse during the stroke but will keep going toward the hole, the same as in a putt. In fact, the chip shot is similar to a putt in most respects. I even bent my left elbow a little when I chipped, and I know some players who use their putting grip for chipping with good results.

It's important to pick a spot on which you want the ball to land. This gives you a definite target at which to aim. Then take the club back low and bring it through low, the same as in putting. You want the ball to roll smoothly once it lands, but if you pick the club up too sharply you'll impart too much backspin. That may cause the ball to bite too quickly or throw it off course.

The stroke itself is made by holding on with the left hand and tapping with the right in a firm-wristed manner. You don't want to be as rigid as a broomstick, so you'll have a little wrist action. But you should never be loose and sloppy with it. Tapping with the right hand gives you a feel for distance—how far you want to carry the ball. But don't forget that the left hand is always in control; it carries directly to the hole and gives direction to your shot. You never, never let that left wrist break down and, as in all other shots, never let the clubhead pass the hands. If you hit behind the ball, or top it, or even hit it cleanly but off line, it's probably because the left hand has quit and the right hand has taken over.

To sum up: your weight is firmly balanced, favoring your heels and your left side. You are slightly open to your target, your club de-lofted. Pick a spot where you want the ball to land. Take the club back with the left hand and tap with the right, making sure the left hand stays firm throughout the stroke. Keep your legs moving and your head still. It's an absolutely foolproof way.

The rest of the shots are hit in almost exactly the same manner. For a pitch-and-run shot from a few yards off the green, just make a slightly bigger swing. If you must loft the ball and put some spin on it—because the pin is close or you have to pitch over a bunker—just open your clubface a bit, and don't put your hands so far ahead at address.

As you move back 25 yards or more from the pin, use much the same stance as you would for any full shot. The important thing to remember is that you must be firm with these shots. Many players have trouble with the half- or three-quarter swing, because they take the club back much too far, then quit on the shot coming through. So if you have half a shot, take half a backswing. If you have a full shot, take a full backswing. And if you have a little shot, take a little backswing. You must practice to learn to judge how far you must take the club back for the various distances. But once you develop a feel for them you'll be able to make firm, effective shots from any distance.

SAND PLAY

The swing you use in getting out of sand is really not much different from the other short shots, but there are a few modifications you must make.

To start with, your stance should be wider than for the normal pitch or chip shot—at least as wide as your shoulders. If your feet are too close together, you'll be inclined to turn and twist too much. The wider stance gives you a much firmer foundation for your swing, and that's all-important in the sand shot. Gary Player, who may be as good a sand player as there is today, is an excellent example of a man who uses a wide stance in the bunker.

You must settle your feet firmly in the sand. If you don't, you'll get the feeling you might slip, and that will subconsciously restrict your swing. You should also make sure there is plenty of flex in your knees, maybe even more than for the normal short shot. This helps you stay down and through, and that's

16. Use a rocking-chair motion in sand

In the sand, your stance should be wider than for a normal pitch or chip shot—at least as wide as your shoulders—and you should use your legs here, too. Think of it as a slight rocking-chair motion with the lower body, but make sure you keep your head very still.

vital in making the sand shot.

Aside from these differences, your stance should be the same as for the chip and pitch—slightly open, weight toward the heels, favoring the left foot. Your clubface, instead of being square and hooded, will be slightly open or pointed right of the target.

The use of the legs is just as important in sand play as it is elsewhere. I like to think of your lower body action in the sand as a rocking-chair motion—feet and knees just rocking slightly from the left to right and left again (see *illustration #16*). Your head *must* stay very still, of course. Your upper body turns rather than swaying back and forth.

For the sand shot, the club is not kept low going back, as it is in chipping or pitching. Instead, you take the club away to the outside of the line, which causes you to pick it up more sharply. Don't physically pick up the club, but make your normal shoulder turn and arm swing, and that outside direction will cause the club to swing on a more upright and steeper arc.

Remember, your goal is not to *blast* the ball from the sand. The mistake most players make is trying to hit too hard in this situation. Instead, try to *slice* the ball from a normal lie in the sand. Think of it as peeling an apple but make sure you don't cut too deeply into it (see *illustration #17*). Aim two inches or so in back of the ball, depending on the consistency of the sand. The swing is firm and not too long, with negligible wrist-break. The left hand and wrist stay firm, as always, but the swing in the sand is controlled largely with the right hand. Use that hand to *cut* the ball out, sliding the clubface under the ball with an outside-to-inside cutting action as you swing through. Don't make the common mistake of chopping down into the sand, because you'll take too much of it and leave the ball in the bunker more times than not.

And don't try to scoop the ball out. Play the ball forward, about opposite your left foot; that way, the clubhead will travel on a more level trajectory as it passes through the sand. And be sure you swing *through*, rather than quitting when you contact the sand. If you do this, the ball will come out of a normal lie high and soft, running very little after it lands.

Make sure you keep your eye on the point at which you want the club to enter the sand, rather than on the ball itself. If

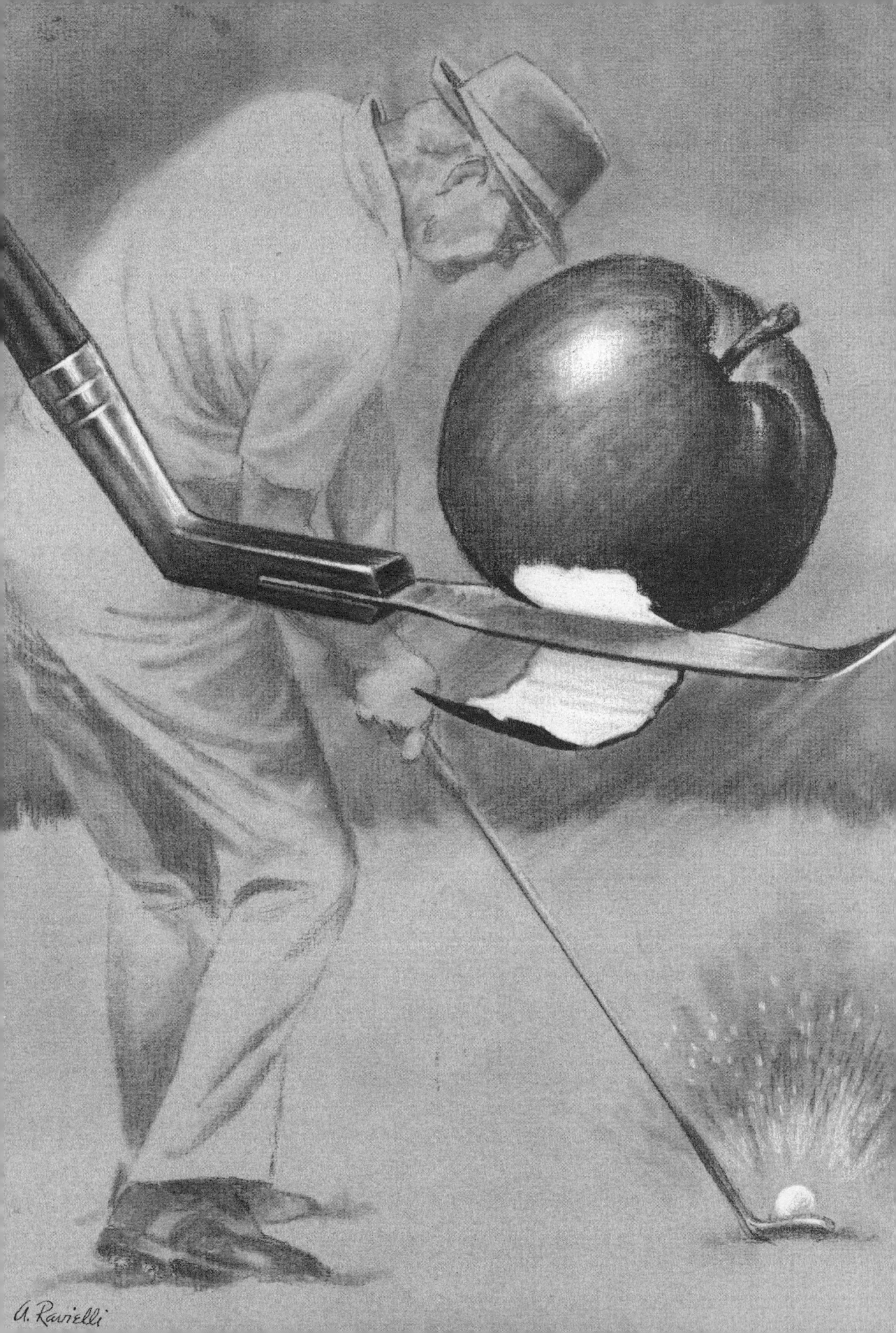

17. Slice the ball from sand
Think of slicing the ball from sand rather than trying to blast it out. Imagine you are slicing an apple without cutting too deeply into the core. Your swing is more upright and slightly to the outside. Use your right hand to cut the ball out with an outside-to-inside cutting action, but be sure your left hand and wrist stay firm. The clubhead should not pass the left hand through the impact area.

you watch the ball, you'll instinctively swing closer to it and are likely to hit the shot thin, blading it over the green.

I always tried to hit the same distance behind the ball, varying the distance of the shot with the length and speed of the swing. You must practice to determine how long and hard to swing for the various distances, but I think you'll find this a more consistent way to play.

For a buried, or "fried-egg" lie, you must square up the clubface to allow the flange (or sole) to cut more deeply into the sand. Aim for the edge of the crater made by the ball and think of cutting that entire crater out of the sand. You may have to swing a little harder, but don't overdo it, because the ball will come out with very little spin and will run farther than normal. If the ball is really buried, you'll have to hit down into the sand with more force and "pop" it out.

There is more than one way to play from sand, of course. Sam Snead, who is a fantastic bunker player, feels the weight should be kept on the left side throughout the swing. Julius Boros, with the great rhythm he has, uses very little body action and just kind of drops the club behind the ball, slapping it out of the sand. Chandler Harper, a former PGA champion, had such a great touch that he almost chipped the ball out of the bunker from a normal lie. Sometimes, if your lie is good and the lip of the bunker is not too high, you might be better off trying that yourself.

I think that if you follow the basic technique I've outlined, and learn to trust it, you'll find that the mysteries of sand play will be solved. With practice, you'll soon be playing from bunkers with confidence and skill.

UNUSUAL LIES AND TROUBLE SHOTS

There are times, of course, when your ball is not going to be sitting up nicely in a level spot on the fairway just waiting for you to strike it smartly with your normal swing. In fact, there probably will be very few times during a round of golf—outside of your 18 tee shots—when that happens. Unless you control your shots better than most of us, you're going to be playing from rough and unusual lies, often under windy conditions and sometimes in the rain.

Meeting the challenge of trouble shots is the test of a golfer. I can't think of a great one who couldn't play out of trouble or overcome unusual situations. Jack Nicklaus, for example, is the best trouble player I've ever seen. If they played every tournament in the rough, Jack would win them all.

Arnold Palmer is great at getting out of trouble, too. Both Jack and Arnold excel at it because they have such tremendous power; in fact, I think the only time power becomes a big asset in golf is when you are playing out of trouble. But that doesn't mean you can't be a good trouble player without being big and strong. Chi Chi Rodriguez, who hardly weighs anything at all, is very good out of trouble. He has such unusual dexterity that he can just pick the ball out and make it do almost anything.

In my time, Jug McSpaden, Jimmy Demaret, and Lawson Little were very fine trouble players, because in addition to being strong they had the ability to maneuver the ball. Johnny Revolta was a great trouble player, too, because he was such a great scrambler.

The ability to recover from trouble depends a lot on attitude. Some players just give up when they hit it into the bushes; either they panic or they take a penalty stroke. Others seem to rise to the occasion and often hit spectacular trouble shots. But I'll warn you that those shots aren't made without preparation. McSpaden, for instance, used to practice hooking and fading the ball, hitting it high and low, and he could make any of these shots with great accuracy. He had a tendency to be wild, and he had to develop his trouble shots because he knew he was going to have a lot of them to play.

You must keep your head about you when you're in trouble. I remember one particular trouble shot I hit that won my second Masters championship for me in 1942. On the 18th tee, I needed a par 4 to tie Ben Hogan, who was already in. It was wet, and in trying to hit the tee shot hard I slipped and pushed it deep into the trees on the right. When I got to the ball, I fortunately found I had room to take a full swing, and there was a small opening in the trees ahead of me. But after the ball came through that opening I was going to have to hook it 40 or 50 feet.

I took a 5-iron and was able to make a fine swing. I kept my eye on the ball, my head still and I didn't worry about where the ball was going to go. So many people, when they are making a shot like this, will look to the opening or to where they want the ball to go just about the time they're making contact. A shot like that will never succeed.

The secret to recovering from problems like the one I've just described is to believe in your swing, believe that what you're trying to do is right, and let the club put the ball where you want it to go.

I did that in the 1942 Masters and the ball went through exactly as it should. It even made the green. I ran my birdie putt over the cup, got my par and won the playoff the next day.

So you should think more about what you must do to execute the problem shot than on what is going to happen to the ball. Strangely enough, if you approach such shots with the attitude that you are going to pull them off, you'll find that, more often than not, you'll be able to concentrate on the swing rather than the result—and therefore execute the shot successfully.

Of course, while attitude is probably the most important factor, certain physical variations must be utilized to make these shots under difficult circumstances. Following is a primer on the three most common problems you'll face and how to solve them.

From rough: For the short pitch from rough around the green, play what is known as a semi-explosion shot, similar to the shot from sand. Using a pitching wedge or sand wedge, open your stance and the blade slightly, and play the ball near the center of your stance. Swing the club up sharply (but don't *pick* it up with your hands) and, using a steeply descending downswing, "cut" the ball out of the grass, swinging through the grass under the ball and letting the cushion of grass lift the ball out (see *illustration #18*). Keep your left hand and wrist firm through impact and be sure to swing *through* the shot. If you don't, the right hand will take over and the shot will be ruined.

A common tendency on these shots is failing to stay down through the shot. Most players want to lift the ball out of trouble rather than letting the loft of the club do it. This only causes them to lift up on the downswing and leave the ball in the heavy grass. So be sure to keep a good knee flex throughout the swing.

The same technique applies to longer shots from rough, except that you try to make club-ball contact as clean as you can rather than cutting the shot out. Again, the swing path is steeper to avoid catching the club in the grass. Your swing should be firm, and your backswing shorter than normal.

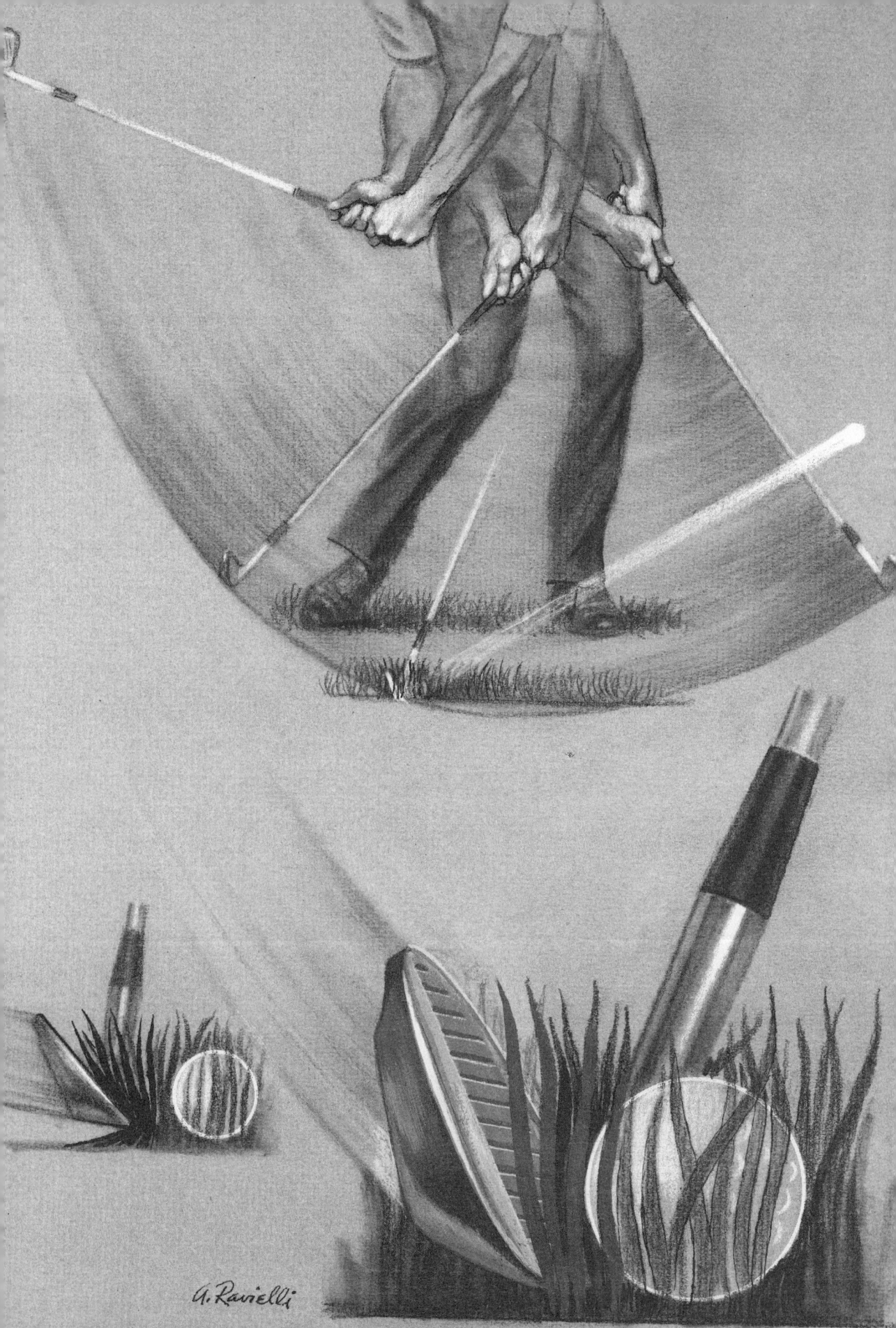

18. Cut the ball out of heavy rough

The short pitch from heavy rough is played as a "semi-explosion" shot, much like the shot from sand. Open your clubface and your stance slightly. Swing the club up more sharply and, using a steeply descending downswing, cut the ball out of the grass. Keep your left hand and wrist firm as you swing through the shot. The clubface actually cuts through the grass under the ball and lifts it out.

Be sure to choose a club with enough loft to get out of the grass—it's seldom advisable to use a long iron out of heavy rough. You're usually in danger with any club longer than a 5-iron. On the other hand, if the grass is not too long, it might be wise to use a 4- or 5-wood and "pop" the ball out. Use the same steep up-and-down swing path and keep the clubface square. Because of its construction, the wood will ride through the grass easier than a long iron, and you'll be able to get good distance on the shot.

The mistake most players make on long rough shots is trying to hit the ball too hard. This usually causes them to swing out of control; they fail to make clean contact and leave the ball in the rough. Concentrate instead on making a smooth swing and getting the ball back in play, even if you have to sacrifice some distance. That smooth swing usually will give you a lot more distance than you might expect.

In the wind: Realizing just one fact will help you become a better wind player—*if you hit the ball solidly, it's amazing how little the wind will affect it.*

If you feel that a headwind or sidewind is so strong that the ball must be kept down, simply use the technique I described earlier for hitting low shots— move the ball back in your stance and be sure to keep your hands ahead. Having learned the hard way in those Texas winds, I also found it advantageous to use at least one longer club than you normally would and swing within yourself, perhaps even easier than usual.

I always found it better to use the wind rather than fight it. In other words, if it's blowing from right to left, aim your shot to the right, hit it normally and let the wind carry it in. Sometimes, if you must hit to a hard green and have little landing area, you can feather the ball in against the wind—fading it against a right-to-left wind, drawing it against a left-to-right breeze. But you had better have the proficiency and confidence in your swing to pull the shot off or you'll end up far off line.

Of course, if the wind is blowing strongly at your back, use a more lofted club than normal and allow for the fact that the ball will run farther than normal after landing.

In wet weather: When playing in the rain or on a wet course, take the usual precautions to keep yourself and your equipment as dry as possible. And remember to play within yourself. The poorer golfer, particularly one who is inexperienced in wet-weather play, tends to panic a bit in such conditions. He'll start swinging out of control with much less effectiveness. Even if he makes contact, he's quite likely to hit "flyers." These shots, which are caused by grass or excess moisture getting between the ball and clubface, ordinarily squirt off the club with less spin, causing the ball to fly erratically or go unusual distances.

Under these circumstances, the good player will realize that, because his clothes are damp, the air is heavy, and his footing probably not as secure, he won't be able to get as much distance on his shots. He'll use more club, grip a little shorter for control, and simply try to make clean contact to avoid those fliers and get the maximum distance possible. He'll overcome the adverse conditions by swinging smoothly and in balance.

I guess that's pretty good advice for any shot you'll ever play on a golf course.

CHECKLIST

So many important points have been covered in chapters 3 through 6 that I'm listing them here for quick review and handy reference. Whenever you feel your game slipping away from you, give yourself a refresher course by going over these important principles:

Chapter 3:
LEARN TO SWING THE MODERN WAY
- In the modern golf swing, ease and comfort are the watchwords. The best way to swing is the simplest way.
- In gripping the club, you should feel pressure in the hands but not in the forearms. Make sure your left-hand grip pressure is dominant.
- For proper aim and alignment, keep a slightly open stance.
- The waggle sets the tempo for the whole swing.
- Begin the takeaway with the left side.
- Don't overswing on the backswing. A longer backswing will not produce longer shots.
- Let your wrists cock gradually and naturally on the backswing.
- On the downswing, the entire left side starts down together, leading the hands and clubhead down, into and through the ball.

Chapter 4:
IMAGES TO MAKE THE MODERN SWING WORK
- Don't be anxious at the top . . . feeling leisurely is a thought that works.
- Keep your arm speed steady in both directions.
- A smooth, unified swing at the right speed gives you proper tempo and maximum power.
- The key to maintaining balance during the swing is to set up properly and keep your head still.
- Keep your knees slightly flexed.
- Be firm but relaxed at the top.
- Let the right elbow swing free.
- Freedom down below keeps the head still.
- Lead downswing with a free left side.
- Swing out from under your head.
- Stay down and through.
- Don't try to *hit* the ball—swing *through it.*

Chapter 5:
SPECIAL THOUGHTS TO DEVELOP POWER AND CONSISTENCY
- Hang on with the left hand for consistency.
- The ideal clubhead path is from inside the target line to along that line during impact.
- Swing the clubhead squarely into the back of the ball.
- Hit from the ball on through.
- Visualize your target.
- The full swing is the same with all clubs.
- Develop a swing you can repeat every time.

Chapter 6:
NEW TECHNIQUES TO MODERNIZE YOUR OLD SHORT GAME
- In putting, never let the putterhead pass the hands.
- Never pick the club up going back or through the putt.
- Keep your eyes over the target line for all putts.
- In putting, roll the ball to the hole.
- *Believe* in the line of travel you pick and let the putter swing along that line.
- On all chip shots and pitches, you must have freedom in the legs.
- Stay slightly open to the target and de-loft the club for all chip shots.
- On sand shots, think of your lower body action as a rocking-chair motion.
- From normal lies in the sand, *slice* the ball out—like peeling an apple.

PART III:
USING YOUR HEAD TO LOWER YOUR SCORE

CHAPTER 7:
THINK YOUR WAY TO SUCCESS

I've listened to many arguments about the mental aspect of golf and its relative importance. Some say the game is 50 percent mental. Others contend that the figure should be 95 percent. The answer probably lies somewhere in between, but I've never known an experienced player or teacher who didn't agree that controlling your mind on the golf course is necessary if you're going to be a successful player.

I'm not denying the importance of developing the correct physical fundamentals and building them into a swing that strikes the ball effectively. You must do it—and with knowledge and practice you can. But at that point all you have is the ability to make reasonably good shots; the world is full of excellent practice-range swingers who can't play a lick once they get to the first tee.

Out there on the course, each shot suddenly means something. If you miss it, you can't just reach for another practice ball and correct your error without penalty. Instead, you must find the ball and play it—and each time you do that a stroke will be marked down and totted up against you at the end of the hole and the round. This realization, even though it may be subconscious, sends most higher handicap players into a state of semi-panic. Even the good players sometimes succumb, especially in moments of extreme pressure.

What you must do is control your mind and nerves to the point where you can take that swing you made so effortlessly on the practice tee and make it work on the first hole—and the second, and the third, and on through the 18th. Not only that, you must be concerned about making good *shots* as well as good *swings*. That involves knowing where to hit the ball, what kind of shot to play under different circumstances and which club you must select to pull it off.

I'm not going to talk at all about club selection and very little about strategy—which shot to hit when and where. As you gain experience, common sense will tell you those things. What I am going to try to do is give you the right mental approach so that you can first make the proper shot-making decisions, then execute them with a good swing.

BE REALISTIC
The first step in building a solid, dependable attitude is to be realistic—not only about your inherent capabilities, but also about how well you are playing to those capabilities on any given day.

Before you do anything else, you must accept the physical abilities you bring to the game and develop these as fully as you can. Never quit trying to improve, of course, but don't try to be something you can't. If you don't have the size and strength to be a long hitter, for example, develop your short-game skills to make up for this.

I think everyone should pattern himself after a good player. If you began playing the game as a youngster, you probably did that subconsciously—and it's still a good idea even if you have waited until adulthood to start playing. But, for heaven's sake, emulate somebody with your own size and physical characteristics. If you're 5'8", don't try to pattern your swing after that of Tom Weiskopf, who is 6'2". If you're a big guy, don't copy Gary Player, because you may not need to do the same things he does, or swing the way he does, to be successful.

Once you have a style of play that works for you, and you're getting everything out of it that you can, make up your mind that this is what you're going to do and play within that framework. I think you'll be amazed at how well you can play, even though your game doesn't resemble Jack Nicklaus' one bit.

Realism must extend to an awareness that you're not going to play the same way every day. Some days your body just doesn't work as well as it does on others. While it's important to always have a positive attitude, you're just fooling yourself if, on those bad days when you're not hitting the ball solidly, you keep selecting clubs you must hit perfectly to reach your target. So, after you've hit a few less-than-satisfactory shots and realize you don't feel as loose and free as usual, adjust your thinking for that day. Take plenty of club and make an easier swing. Even though you may not hit the shot perfectly, you'll begin to reach the green.

The same philosophy applies all the way through your game. Suppose you're having a stretch of trouble with your chipping. Until you can get to the practice green and work it out, why not putt the ball from the fringe if the area is smooth enough? The pros do. They're not too proud to use the most effective club in a given situation, so you shouldn't be, either. In other words, I go right back to the fact that you shouldn't try something you can't do well, whether it be a temporary or permanent situation.

Also, we all get older year by year, and since I'm now a senior golfer I can speak

109

from experience. I find the biggest problem with the older player is that he isn't aware—or won't admit—that his muscles aren't as supple as they used to be. He doesn't have as much swing motion and he isn't getting the distance on his shots that he once did.

So, seniors, do some stretching exercises and loosen up a little longer before you play, and practice a little more if you can. Above all, fit your game to what you've got going for you at the moment. At one time you might have been able to get home with a 5-iron from 175 yards, but now it might take a 5-wood. Use the 5-wood. Who cares, as long as it gets there? Be realistic about your capabilities *now* and you'll retain your ability to play well for just about as long as you want.

PLAY WITHIN YOURSELF

The expression, "play within yourself," is heard often, but what does it really mean? In a broad sense, it means just what I've been telling you: establish a realistic style of play and don't try to exceed your limitations. To give it a more practical definition, avoid hitting each shot so hard that your swing goes out of control. Make each swing with something less than an all-out effort.

There are times, I suppose, when you must try to get extra distance on a shot—a drive that must get around the corner of a dogleg, a 3-wood shot that must carry a lake if you are to win the hole or the match. Unfortunately, our instincts tell us to try to hit the ball much harder than we would under normal circumstances. When we do, all sorts of bad things happen. We swing too fast, which actually shortens the swing; we hit too early from the top of the swing; we hit too much with the right hand; and we hit behind the ball or on top of it. We never time or coordinate the swing properly, and as a result the shot loses both distance and accuracy.

Distance is the intimidator that usually causes the overly hard, fast swing. If you'll think about it, you rarely swing a 9-iron too hard, but you almost always swing a driver too hard. Even the good players do it, especially when they're playing on an extra-long course.

A few years ago at the Masters I visited with Billy Casper, who had often commented that he didn't play the Augusta National course well. But I had observed him and knew his game. I figured there was no reason he shouldn't play the course well enough to win the Masters championship. Because I liked

Billy Casper had for years talked himself out of the Masters until, in 1970, he decided to "play within himself." He concentrated on swinging at his normal tempo and, as a result, won the championship that year after defeating Gene Littler in a thrilling playoff.

Billy, I took it upon myself to question him about it.

It turns out that he believed too much of what he read in the papers about Augusta National being a long hitter's course, and as soon as he got there every spring his swing tempo changed. Billy is a beautiful driver and fairway wood player, but at Augusta National he tried to hit the ball harder and farther than he normally does. As a result, he would subconsciously speed up his swing. That caused him to hit the ball less solidly and with less distance than usual.

I pointed this out to Billy and as soon as he realized what he was doing he began playing within himself. The next year, he won the championship.

How to play within yourself is a problem, and I'd be lying to you if I said I had the magic formula. Not only does the problem of distance cause you to hit harder, but pressure also makes you speed up your swing. I have a thought or two that should help here.

Be aware that when the going gets rough, and you're getting a little nervous about winning the Nassau bet or the match in your club tournament, the last thing you want is to speed up your tempo and destroy your rhythm. Actually, you want to *tone down* your swing instead of *toning it up*. Relax your muscles, slow down your backswing, but keep it rhythmic; reach a little more going back; get a little more stretch; and move *smoothly* into the forward swing. Convince yourself that the smooth, relaxed swing will send the ball as far—usually farther—than a hard, fast swing. That's what I mean by playing within yourself.

It's easier said than done, of course, and requires a lot of self-discipline. But program your mind to do it; you'll be better off for it.

DON'T THINK ABOUT MECHANICS

In the early stages of my career I thought a lot about mechanics. Was I taking the club straight back on line? How high were my hands going on the backswing? How was I going to start down? I'm sure these questions occurred because I was making such major changes in my swing at that time. However, most players never get beyond that stage.

Then, from about 1937 on through the rest of my career, I didn't think about much while making a shot. I had developed a style of play which I used all through this period. It became pretty automatic and effortless. I had a target in mind and I just visualized the line on which I wanted to take the club away from the ball, and the line on which I wanted to return it.

That was the thought that triggered my swing. You might have a different key thought. Realistically, you might even have two swing thoughts—a backswing thought and a downswing thought, perhaps. These thoughts should be programmed as much as possible into your subconscious before you swing—they should be almost instinctive rather than a conscious process of the mind.

Bob Jones hit the nail on the head when he said that when he was thinking about three things during his swing he was playing poorly; when he was thinking about two things he had a chance to shoot par; and when he was thinking of only one thing he figured he could win the tournament.

If you can play that way, your results are going to be much better than the person who has to think about his swing step-by-step. That's why a golfer practices—to get to the point where he doesn't have to think about the physical execution of his shot. You must develop enough confidence in your swing so you can trust it completely. The only way to do that is to hit enough good shots until you know you can make them without consciously analyzing each one.

Once you've developed that kind of confidence—where you can execute the swing with your subconscious—then all you have to think about is the shot itself and what is required: Where do I want it to land? Do I want to hit it high or low? With a fade or a draw? I won't tell you that developing the confidence to make this kind of automatic swing is easy, but striving for it is worthwhile, because this is what it takes to become a good player.

PLAY DECISIVELY

Golf is like life in many ways. For example, when you make a decision, you should stick with it. I've talked with a lot of business executives who have to make pretty quick decisions in some important matters, and they tell me their first decision nearly always is the right one. If they spend too much time thinking it over they often become confused and end up making the wrong decision.

The same thing is true on the golf course. You must play decisively. Once you choose how to play a shot and what club to use, don't change that decision unless some unusual circumstance forces you to.

Very seldom will you see players like Jack Nicklaus or Gary Player or Billy Casper take a club out of the bag, put it back in and then pull out another one. They'll look at a shot, make the decision, pull out the club and go! Lee Trevino is another good example. Once he makes up his mind, he doesn't deviate. As a matter of fact, when he has a difficult shot under tight conditions, he plays extremely fast—sometimes so fast in an important tournament that the television cameraman will miss the shot.

So be decisive. That attitude is particularly important in putting. Look at the line of a putt, decide how much it will break and how hard you want to hit it, then make the stroke. I've seen very few players get set over a putt, back off, change their minds, and then make the putt.

BE AGGRESSIVE

When I was a boy learning to play golf, missing the green with your approach shot meant you were supposed to be content with a bogey. Today, the best golfers don't buy that approach. If they get into trouble, they'll fight and scratch and scramble to get out, and very often they will somehow come up with a par.

Arnold Palmer, in his familiar putting crouch, sinks another long one. Palmer's positive approach to the game has been a major factor in his successful career.

That's the attitude you should take onto the course all the time. I don't mean that you should be foolish about it and take chances when you don't have to. Play within yourself. But don't play defensively or hesitantly. *Think that you're going to hit each shot well instead of trying not to hit it badly.*

Don't be looking for trouble. Look instead for a successful shot. If you come to a par-5 that you can reach in two shots, even if it's a little tight, take out your driver and have a good swing at it. If you're shooting at the green, don't just wish the shot up there, hoping it gets on. Try to make it come down right on top of the flag.

If you have a long putt, don't approach it with the hope that you won't three-putt. With that negative attitude, you usually will fail. Instead, tell yourself that you're going to roll it right to the hole. If you have a putt within a makeable range, don't think about missing it. *Expect* the ball to go in the hole. I'll swear that Arnold Palmer in his prime used to *will* his putts into the hole. Johnny Miller has said that when he's putting well he feels the same way. And I'm sure that's the way Jack Nicklaus approaches his putts, particularly the crucial ones.

Sometimes you must be more aggressive than usual. If you're behind in your Sunday morning match or in a tournament, you'll have to take some chances. You'll have to fire at the flag even if it's tucked behind a bunker. You might try a long carry over trouble or maybe even a miracle recovery shot that you wouldn't ordinarily attempt. You must make sure you get the ball to the hole, especially on the makeable putts.

Even if you're leading a tournament, or have two sides of the Nassau won, or are heading for your best score ever, you should rarely forego your aggressive attitude and start playing defensively. That doesn't mean you should take a lot of risks, but you should stay on the attack with a positive attitude. If you turn defensive and try to protect your lead or your score, not only do you give other players a chance to catch you, but your own play usually begins to suffer. Once you lose that aggressive attitude, it's hard to regain it.

STRATEGY IS THINKING

I'll close this chapter on "thinking golf" by telling you again to do just that—think! Using your head is what course strategy is all about. Be aware of course

conditions. Are the greens hard or soft? Wet or dry? How is the wind blowing? The answers to these questions will guide you in your club selection and tell you how you must play each of your shots.

Know where the pins are placed. That knowledge tells you *where* you must place your shots—not only into the green but also off the tee to set up that shot to the flag. Know where the trouble is and what you must do to stay away from it.

I had a good year in 1944. In fact, I had a 69.67 stroke average, which was the lowest on record at the time. But I wasn't satisfied with myself at all. I had kept a diary during the season, and after each round I had written notes in my little black book on things I felt I needed to work on. At the end of the year I took inventory, looking for trends in my play that should be countered. I found that frequently I'd been guilty of bad thinking. I'd gotten sloppy with a little ol' putt, or I'd had a good score going but had eased up and not played a shot for what it was worth. Sometimes I'd be three or four under par—really sailing along—and I'd come to an open driving hole and wouldn't pay enough attention to where I wanted the ball to land. I wouldn't make a bad swing—it seemed like I couldn't make a bad swing during that streak—but I hadn't thought about the shot enough, and sometimes it got me in trouble.

I made a couple of small mechanical changes at the time, mostly to improve my chipping. But the main thing I did was determine that I wasn't going to waste a single shot because of poor thinking. The result was that in 1945 I got my stroke average down more than a shot a round.

I don't imagine you can reduce your scoring average to 68.33, as I did, but I will promise you that better thinking can take even more than a stroke per round off your score.

CHAPTER 8: LEARN THE TWO Cs— CONCENTRATION AND COMPOSURE

Every great player has learned the two Cs: how to *concentrate* and how to maintain *composure*. If you really want to learn them, the two Cs aren't difficult to master.

Let's start with concentration. That simply means paying attention so closely to what you're doing that outside interruptions don't bother you. If you've watched the better players in professional tournaments, you may have noticed that most noises, including roars from the crowd on a nearby hole, don't disturb them. It really takes some unusually loud or startling noise close by to make them step back from a shot.

Another factor in concentration that doesn't show is the ability to shut off interference from your own thought processes. That's even more difficult than blocking out noise. It's a matter of training and, as usual, there is no easy way to do it. You must train your mind to react the same way you teach your muscles to react subconsciously during a golf swing—by practice. You simply tell yourself that you're going to keep your attention trained on what you're doing and not notice any distractions. Pretty soon you'll notice them less and less.

Of course, you must think positively about what you are doing. This is the biggest aid in eliminating outside distractions and the tendency to let your mind wander to other things while you're playing. Every time you sense this interference, either from outside or within, think instead about playing the shot at hand. You'll be amazed at how soon you begin to block out those distractions and go on to play the shot successfully.

When I was playing, we didn't have television. But we had movie cameras that followed us around on trucks and made all sorts of noise. It drove some of the players up a wall. When I first started playing they bothered me, too, but I convinced myself that those noises were always going to be there and I might as well get used to them. So even though I heard the noise, I'd go ahead and play, and before long it didn't bother me in the least. I had trained my subconscious not to let it affect me. I wasn't any smarter than anybody else, but I did have enough judgment to know that the more I could ignore this obvious distraction, the less trouble I'd have with any interference during the course of play.

Maintaining concentration was even harder for a tournament professional in my time than it is now, because the fans were so close to us. We didn't have gallery ropes, and they would walk down the fairway with us and talk with us. I might talk to them, but I'd be so into what I was doing that I might answer them and not even know it. It's like being absorbed in reading a book when somebody asks you a question. You might answer them, but you really didn't hear them. That's the same type of concentration you have to develop on the golf course.

I don't mean that you shouldn't talk to your playing partners, because in most cases you're just playing a sociable game. But if you really want to play well, you must learn to shut out their conversation and all other distracting influences while you are in the process of planning and making each shot.

It's also important, particularly if you're playing in a tournament, to pay the strictest attention to your own game and not be influenced by what your playing partners are doing. How many times when watching a professional tournament do you see a threesome in which everybody is either several strokes under par or several strokes over? Quite often—and the reason is that most players tend to get carried along by somebody else's momentum.

I guess it's all right to let yourself be influenced by a member of your group who is playing well, but by leaving yourself open to this kind of influence you also risk being dragged down by the playing partner who is doing poorly. In the long run, you're better off taking care of yourself and not paying so much attention to how everyone else is playing.

That philosophy is especially important in match play, where you are going against an opponent head-to-head. It's easy to worry about his game more than yours. And if you happen to get a few holes up on him, it's even easier to become complacent. You might even start to sympathize with him, and that can be disastrous! I remember how, in the years when we had a lot of match-play tournaments, I'd get an opponent two or three holes down, start to feel sorry for him, and unconsciously slack off in my own play. The first thing I knew he'd have me by the seat of the pants and I was beaten. It didn't take me long to get over that attitude, and it's something you should work to avoid.

Keeping your composure is a matter of accepting what comes along and not letting it bother you. That's difficult enough in everyday living, I know. It's particularly hard on the golf course, because we all feel we should play a little better than we really do. But if you don't keep your composure, you have no chance to turn in a good score at the end of the round.

To start with, you can't let a bad shot or a bad hole bother you. You must forget about it. It's gone, like yesterday, and there's not a thing in the world you can do about it. You can't get angry at yourself or start belittling yourself. You can't say, "Aw, you stupid jerk, why in the world did you do that?" Once you start thinking that way, you'll start believing it. You'll dwell on it, and then you'll start to make more mistakes, one bad shot after another. Don't go too far the other way either. After you've made a bogey or double-bogey, don't march to the next tee determined that you must get a birdie to make up for it. That just puts added pressure on you, and chances are you won't be able to handle it.

Above all, don't feel that just because you've missed a shot or two (or three) you've lost your game. Accept the fact that you're human and are going to make a lot of mistakes. More than that, realize that you're really going to hit very few shots perfectly during the course of a round. I've heard Ben Hogan say that he never played a round in his life in which he hit more than four or five shots that he was satisfied with. Hogan also said that golf is a game of mistakes, and the object is to keep your bad shots straight and in play.

I think Jack Nicklaus is the greatest thinker on the golf course I've ever seen—even better than Hogan, who was a great one. I've seen Nicklaus miss some shots, maybe flub a little chip shot and look awfully bad. Then he'll step up, without much time in between, and hit a beautiful shot. That's composure.

One good tip that can help you keep your composure is *don't rush*. I learned that lesson early in my tournament career. As I've mentioned, there were no ropes along the fairways and so the gallery walked with us. You'd hit a shot and the fans would rush to get in position to watch the next one. It was easy to get carried along by them, and pretty soon you'd be walking too fast and playing too fast. I learned to be aware of this and would consciously slow myself down.

That's even more important when you're under pressure, because you naturally tend to speed up at such times. The best advice then, whenever you start getting excited, or you're angry over a missed shot, is to slow down. I don't mean that you should dally and waste time, but slow yourself down to a normal relaxed pace.

You should also slow down your breathing in times of stress. *Breathe*

Jack Nicklaus, who is probably the greatest thinker on the golf course that the game has ever known, lines up a shot with his usual fierce concentration.

deeply. It's an excellent way to relieve tension and get your mind back on what you're doing. As a matter of fact, it's good to get in the habit of taking a deep, slow breath before every shot, particularly when you are putting.

These physical remedies will help, but controlling your nerves remains something that, in the long run, you must do with your mind. Everybody gets nervous in crucial situations. The possibility of winning or losing a $2 bet is just as crucial to you as the prospect of winning the U.S. Open was to me. Everybody—you, me, Jack Nicklaus—feels pressure, and it's a difficult thing to overcome. On the professional tour, I see very few players leading a tournament at some stage for the first time who go on to win it. The pressure gets them. So don't be upset when you feel those butterflies in your stomach. Admit that you're nervous, that you're feeling pressure. Don't try to ignore it, because you can't. Instead, try to do something about it. Frank Beard once said everybody feels pressure; it's when you succumb to it that you choke.

To control your nerves, you must have a positive thought in your mind. You must think about what must be done to make a successful shot instead of worrying about missing it. Of course, you must have confidence in your ability to make the shot required. This comes, as I've said, from practice. It also comes easier after you've been in a few pressure situations and have learned to handle them. There is no substitute for experience, and the more you learn to react properly under pressure, the better you'll be able to perform the next time.

I guess the best way to avoid getting uptight is to be realistic about yourself. Realize you're going to hit some shots well and some badly. You'll win some matches and lose some. It really isn't the end of the world either way. Even the professionals who make their living at the game have to think this way. It is, especially for you, just a game. If you'll convince yourself that the next crucial shot you have to hit is not the most important thing you'll ever do, you'll be much more relaxed and able to execute the shot.

Composure comes from within. All the things I've told you in this chapter are aimed at helping you come to terms with yourself as a golfer. When you do, you'll find composure and the game will be more fun. You'll also play better.

CHAPTER 9: WHAT MAKES A CHAMPION

The title of this chapter might be misleading—except that I think you're realistic enough to know I'm not necessarily talking about being champion of the U. S. Open or the Masters or the Professional Golfers' Association. Everything I'm going to say is representative of those champions, but it also applies to champions at every other level. Everybody wants to be a champion, even if it's of his own Sunday foursome.

There's really nothing magical about being a champion. *A champion is someone who is willing to work harder and give more than his peers*. He devotes more of himself to the task. He is fulfilling a passionate desire to be better, a desire from inside that continues to build.

You've heard the old saying that an athlete always plays better when he's hungry. Well, that doesn't always mean hungry literally. Jack Nicklaus isn't worried any more about making a lot of money, but he's still hungry to win the Grand Slam, to add to the major championships that he's won, to do more than anyone else has ever done. I always had something in mind other than winning a particular tournament. I wanted to win every tournament in this country. At least once I wanted to win the Vardon Trophy for low scoring average; I wanted to get on the Ryder Cup team; and I wanted to be the leading money-winner. I always had some sort of goal like that in front of me, and I think every good player does. Your goals may be more modest, but you must have something to aim for or you won't have the incentive to play better.

I've been accused of being a perfectionist, and I guess I am. Everything I've done I've wanted to do as well as I possibly could. I think you have to have this attitude to achieve any kind of success. A good player loves to compete, loves to win and hates to lose. You show me a good loser and I'll show you somebody who doesn't win much.

It's understood that to be a winner you must develop a golf swing in which you have confidence, one that will hold up and work for you under pressure. But it doesn't stop there. From that point you have to keep working on your game, keep trying for improvement. If somebody is beating you pretty regularly in your weekend group, there's only one way to turn that around—you must learn to play better than he does. It's that simple.

You don't need to spend a lot of time at

it either. The more the better, of course, but not many amateurs can devote as much time as they should to practice and improvement. But if you have proper direction and use your practice time wisely, you can improve rapidly. Your professional can give you specific help if you feel you need it, but you can help yourself immensely, simply by knowing what areas to work on and how.

You must work on the parts of your game that are troubling you, of course. But I think most of your practice should be with the 8-iron down through the wedge, and of course your sand play and putting. In the first place, a good short game can cut most of the strokes off your score. Secondly, hitting pitch shots of 40 to 60 yards is a great way to develop your rhythm and tempo. You're swinging the club so slowly that you can feel the swing much better than on a harder, faster swing with a long club.

When I left the tour in 1946 I played hardly at all until I played in the Crosby tournament early in 1951. In preparing for it, I realized I had to get my rhythm back, so when I practiced I didn't hit any shot longer than 100 yards. That way I could feel what I was doing with my swing. And it paid off in two ways. Besides getting my tempo back, I pitched the ball absolutely perfectly during the tournament—and I won it.

So instead of slugging out a few quick practice shots with a driver before you play, as most golfers are inclined to do, hit some shorter shots to get that feel and rhythm going. Then hit a couple of longer shots to stretch your muscles a bit.

Incidentally, pre-round practice should be only for warm-up. You really shouldn't work on correcting any swing problems, because if you do your mind will be too cluttered when you get to the first tee. Instead, try to plan your pre-round activities so you don't have to rush. Walk to the practice tee and warm up with some leisurely short shots—and I stress *leisurely*. It's easy to develop too fast a swing tempo on the practice range, and that carries right over onto the course.

If you're having trouble with your game, the time to work on it is after the round. But don't try to correct things beforehand or on the course.

THE KEY TO GOOD PRACTICE HABITS

In practicing, there's a good way to decide if your work is effective and you are hitting the ball solidly. A number of times before a tournament even started

I'd tell my wife I was going to win the tournament. When she asked me how I knew, I'd tell her it was because I was hitting the ball exactly the same length every time.

That's a key a lot of people aren't aware of. Watch your caddie when you're hitting balls to him; or if you don't have a caddie, pick out a spot where the balls are landing. They might vary a little right or left, but if they are landing out there the same distance every time, it means you're swinging well and hitting the ball solid. That's when you can start believing in your swing.

Practice is a funny thing, because a human being is a funny machine. You must practice and play to improve, yet there are times when you can do both too much. If you are playing well, for instance, I wouldn't spend a lot of time practicing, because you can practice yourself out of a good swing as well as into one. Just hit enough balls to stay limber and in the groove.

If you're playing badly, you must do some work on the practice tee, but there are times when even that doesn't do any good. You continue to play badly and practice badly, and you get more and more frustrated. At those times, simply lay off for a while. That advice might not apply to the player who gets out only once or twice a week, but if you are a more regular golfer in a slump, getting away from the game often is the best remedy.

Don't stay away too long— just a few days, until you're keen to play again. Then you can come back fresh and relaxed, and often this will solve a lot of your problems.

Finally, don't forget the mental aspect of practice. Most people think the only time you're learning golf is on the practice tee, but I don't agree with that at all. I think I've done more for myself—and I've talked to other good players who feel the same—by getting off by myself and just thinking about my game. Maybe after you've gone to bed at night you lie there and get a picture of your swing in your mind. Somehow things are a little clearer to you at those times and you can get a better perspective of the errors you've been making and the correct swing that you do want to execute. I think some of the best lessons I've had in my life came while I was lying in bed at night just thinking about my game.

You might think it strange that a good player would be so worried about his game that he'd lie awake nights thinking about it. That's why he's a good player. He puts in more time and effort than his buddies, and he does better because of that.

One mark of a true champion that is not often discussed is that *he never plays a careless shot*. Jack Nicklaus and Gary Player come quickest to mind as examples of this. I don't think I've ever seen either of them play a shot carelessly, whether it was for a 2 or a 7. This is advisable for anybody, but a champion *has* to have this attitude. Not only can throwing away one or two shots make the difference between winning and losing, but carelessness breeds more carelessness—and pretty soon your tendency is to play that way.

There are some pretty good players around today who, when they realize they're not going to win a hunk of money, just fill out the round. They're not the real champions. In the long run they just hurt themselves. It sounds almost trite to say never give up, or never get careless, but this may be more important in golf than anything else. So much can happen during the course of a round or a tournament to reverse things that a player is silly if he quits.

That ties in with believing in your own ability. You won't ever give up if you have that belief, and you must have it if you are to win. You simply must tell yourself that you're going to play as well as you can and that this effort will be good enough to beat the other player. If you give your best and are beaten, don't get down on yourself. Tell yourself that next time you'll make some putts and maybe your opponent won't. Perhaps the strongest ingredient in the make-up of a champion is precisely that kind of patience. Without it, you'll simply be frustrated—because seldom do things happen exactly how and when you want them to. I was short on patience, because I wanted things to happen too quickly, and I had to learn to control that.

So must you. No one can take a lesson, hear four or five things from his professional and go out on the golf course and put them all into play. If you do try, you'd better not be playing for much money that day. By the same token, you can't read this book and decide you're going to be an instant whiz.

So, take it a bit slower. Work to improve. Believe in yourself and in your ability to improve. Be patient. Success in golf is not quickly or easily achieved, but if you have the knowledge and the desire to work toward it, in time it will come.

EPILOGUE: WHAT HAS HAPPENED AND WHAT LIES AHEAD

I have to admit that I did not foresee the tremendous growth golf has enjoyed. I never dreamed the sport would be as big as it is today. I guess that's because I didn't foresee the amount of leisure time that the average person would have.

A lot of growth factors couldn't be predicted back in my time. I'm referring to such things as the advent of the affluent society after World War II; the awareness of golf to the masses that the late President Eisenhower brought to the game, the growth of television and its coverage of golf; the magnetic popularity of Arnold Palmer. I even like to think that Ben Hogan, Sam Snead and myself, along with some of the other stars of my time, have also influenced the game's growth.

More women and youngsters are playing. This is a healthy thing, and to me it's a sign that the game is going to stay healthy and continue to grow. For golf is played in a healthy environment. I don't know many kids who play a lot of golf and who also get in much trouble. I guess you can say that about all sports, but golf is a game that anyone can play, regardless of size or sex.

Television, of course, makes golf more enjoyable to watch. While the TV people have had their problems, I really believe golf telecasting is getting better. The use of more mobile cameras and more knowledgeable players as commentators has been the biggest improvement; I think we're going to see more of this kind of good work by the television industry.

The product it covers—mainly the professional tour—has never looked healthier. I think the total purse money has been stabilized at about $9 million. The schedule has been shortened, too, and leaves more room for a world-wide tour, which I think we're going to see in the near future.

The tour players, as a group, are becoming more aware of their image and their responsibility to the public. I think almost all of them are genuinely interested in the good of the game. They realize that the fans pay the freight, spending big money for spots in the pro-am events and buying the tickets that result in such great contributions to charities across the country.

The fans keep coming, in ever-growing numbers, and well they should, because today's great players put on quite a show. I really enjoy watching them. For me, it's still a thrill, even after all these years, to follow the tour—the showcase of golf. The game has become so big that golf stars are genuine sports heroes now, and more and more kids are emulating them. That can only be good for the game and its growth.

Nor are we about to run out of stars. Arnold Palmer still captures the galleries, and Jack Nicklaus, Lee Trevino and Gary Player are going strong. There's a new batch of attractive young standouts coming right along behind them. Johnny Miller, of course, will continue to improve, and I am very high on Tom Watson, who may be the next super-star. He's a very long hitter. He plays the good courses well and has proved that he can win in major competition. He also has the personality and appeal that a star must have. John Mahaffey and Tom Kite are cast in the same mold—they all have a chance to become our next great players.

A few dark spots appear in golf's picture, of course. Slow play is one of them. The tour players and everyone else are going to have to speed their pace or the game will be strangled. The five-hour round must be reduced to four or less or else today's faster-moving generation of youngsters will begin turning to other recreational activities.

I'm saddened by the fact that the caddie is a dying breed. Caddying is not only a healthy way to earn money, it's a natural way for a boy to acquire an interest in playing the game. But golf programs are beginning to grow in high schools and colleges, and enlightened golf professionals across the country are starting to conduct clinics for juniors. Moreover, golf has achieved such stature, not only as a potentially lucrative profession, but as an accepted avocation, that the caddie ranks are really no longer necessary as a springboard to playing the game.

I feel very fortunate that I've been able to stay close to the game and grow along with it. Except for playing, I'm more active in golf now than I've ever been in my life, even though I'm 64 years old.

In that regard, my work as a television commentator with ABC has been a tremendous boost for me. I'm recognized by more people now than I ever was as a champion player. Stewardesses on airplanes, waitresses in restaurants, the cabbie on the road, the man on the street—all speak to me as if they know me first-hand. And I think that's marvelous. I never dreamed that it would be anything like this.

So even though I retired 30 years ago, at what most people feel was the peak of my career, I've never had any regrets. Golf has continued to be a major part of my life, and I'm thankful for it.

Golf obviously is an important part of your life, too—and if this book can help it become an even better part, why, that will make me very happy.

BYRON NELSON'S CAREER RECORD

Most victories, one season: 18 in 1945
Most consecutive
 victories, one season: 11 in 1945
Most consecutive times
 top money winner: 113
Lowest scoring average,
 one season: 68.33 in 1956
Athlete of the Year: 1944 and 1945

MAJOR TOURNAMENTS

Masters   Winner, 1937, 1942; runner-up, 1941; tied for second, 1947
U.S. Open   Winner, 1939; tied for first, 1946 (lost to Lloyd Mangrum in playoff)
PGA   Winner, 1940, 1945; runner-up, 1939, 1941, 1944

VICTORIES, YEAR BY YEAR

1930   Southwest Amateur
1936   Metropolitan Open
1937   Masters, Belmont, Thomasville, Central Pennsylvania Opens
1938   Thomasville, Hollywood Opens
1939   U.S. Open, Western, North and South, Phoenix, Massachusetts Opens
1940   PGA, Texas, Miami, Ohio Opens
1941   Miami, Greensboro, Ohio, All-American Opens, Seminole Pro-Am.
1942   Masters, All-American, Oakland, Ohio Opens, Charles Riv. Inv.
1943   Kentucky Open
1944   All-American, San Francisco, Knoxville, Red Cross, Golden Valley, Beverly Hills, Nashville Opens
1945   See separate listing.
1946   Los Angeles, San Francisco, New Orleans, Chicago Victory Opens, Houston and Columbus Inv.
1948   Texas PGA
1951   Bing Crosby Invitational
1955   French Open

1945

Event	Score	Place
Los Angeles Open	284	2
Phoenix Open	274	1
Tucson Open	269	2
Texas Open	269	2
Corpus Christi Open	264	1
New Orleans Open*	284	1
Gulfport Open	275	2
Pensacola Open	274	2
Jacksonville Open	275	T-6
Miami Four Ball**		1
Charlotte Open	272	1
Greensboro Open	271	1
Durham Open	276	1
Atlanta Open	263	1
Montreal Open	268	1
Philadelphia Inquirer Inv.	269	1
Chicago Victory National Open	275	1
PGA Championship***		1
Tam O'Shanter Open	269	1
Canadian Open	280	1
Memphis Invitational	276	T-5
Knoxville Invitational	276	1
Nashville Invitational	269	2
Dallas Open	281	3
Tulsa Open	288	4
Spokane Open	266	1
Portland Invitational	275	2
Tacoma Open	283	T-10
Seattle Open	259	1
Fort Worth Open	273	1

 * Playoff: Nelson 65: McSpaden 70
 ** Won with Harold McSpaden over Denny Shute and Sam Byrd, 8 and 6
 *** Beat Sam Byrd, 4 and 3, in finals.

Clinton F. Loeffler
May 1977